Undefeated
Marketing

How to Avoid 94 Mistakes & Right Hooks and K.O Competitors

Zak Mustapha

Copyright

ISBN-13: 978-1523920587
ISBN-10: 1523920580

Table of Contents

Download the Bonuses

Make sure you download the 13+ bonus materials that include worksheets, checklists and other stuff to help you on your journey.
Get them at
http://www.foolishnessfile.com/undefeated-marketing-bonus.

ABOUT THE AUTHOR

Zak Mustapha is the founder of Foolishness File, a startup that focuses on educating the business community on people's mistakes so they can avoid falling in the same holes.

ACKNOWLEDGEMENTS

I'd like to thank my parents, my sister, the rest of my family and friends for being there for me.

I would also like to thank Joanna Jast (www.shapeshiftersclub.com) and everyone else that supported me along the way.

Don't just flick to the next page, this isn't an ordinary book.

Be honest with me, it's difficult isn't it? The competition is unbearable to say the least. In fact, I always wonder... where the hell did all these business people come from? It's just too crowded.

But, let's put complaining about the competition aside for a second... why did I write this book? It all started with failure. 100% straight failure. Misguided, uninformed... didn't know what to do... didn't know what the hell I was doing.

The first business class I've ever had was in grade 9 and although I got to learn a few definitions such as the marketing mix, acquisitions and economies of scale... it just wasn't enough for the real world. So, I failed...

Undefeated Training
After months of continuous work and dedication, I would wake up to work... sleep, so I can work... eat to work... everything in my life was about my work... yet, everything failed to work. Later on, it struck me... my

equation wasn't complete. I had a missing piece of the puzzle that I had forgotten... no wonder I failed!

All this time I'd been following the old equation most beginners relied on...

Hard work = Success

But, hard work does not equal Success!

The missing piece was "useful knowledge", not just any knowledge... but useful knowledge. The true path to success is knowing and then action. The equation would look like this;

Useful Knowledge + Hard work = Success

That's how boxers train for a fight. They study their opponents' moves, identify weaknesses, create a strategy to beat them and work hard on their strategy.

Due to all my failures... I wrote this book. I knew that wise people learn from their mistakes but wiser people learn from other's mistakes because they know that life is too short to fall into every hole that comes in their way.

Who's this for?

Entrepreneurs who want to succeed in the business world. Entrepreneurs who want to see their ideas become a reality and succeed in the marketplace. Entrepreneurs who have a product but struggle with the rough competition. Most importantly, it's for those who are motivated not just to read theory but ready to take action upon what they learn. If you're reading this book just to learn theory, then put it back – this is not a book for you.

This book is for those who are ready to take their product into the marketplace. They understand that with the technology they have, they can compete with 9-figure budgets, and that large companies were built by people just like themselves and that they can do it too. Yes, I'm talking about YOU. You're still reading because that describes you, because your thoughts were imprinted on this page.

Leaves me with one question;

Do you want to be the Undefeated Marketer?

INTRODUCTION

So you want to beat all the existing champions? Well, you got to train hard!

And not only that... you have to know how others lost, why they lost and how you can avoid it to become the unbeatable champion. I mean, you don't want to lose... do you?

I have to be honest... it's not easy.

But, with this book, it will be a heck lot easier than going alone. In fact, if you follow what I say and work harder than everyone else – you will get there.

Before I tell you about the framework for this book, I want to tell you something real quick...

You see those people who boast about their years of experience? They remind me of a quote by Oscar Wilde who said, "Experience is simply the name we give our mistakes."

What that means is... the more mistakes you learn from, the more experience you gain. So, don't let ANYONE scare you away with their "years" of experience – it doesn't mean a THING!

You see... most people are lazy, even the "hard" workers are lazy. They drag themselves through the same boring routine job for 6 – 8 hours a day and learn nothing more than what you and I can learn in an hour. By learning from the "experiences" or mistakes of successful people, we can accumulate several years of experience ahead of our time. Now, let me tell you how this book is structured and the reason behind structuring it this way.

FIRST, I put General Marketing as the first chapter so you can build the foundations for your product and business, as well as learn principles that will help differentiate you from the competition – or as I like to say, "Make the competition irrelevant".

SECOND, after building a general background in marketing, I knew that most entrepreneurs work towards building a website since it is the home and HQ for most businesses in todays "techy" world. So, I put conversion marketing as the second chapter to help guide that process of building the website.

THIRD, since a website (and all marketing) is useless without any content, I made Direct-Response/content marketing as the third chapter. It is also the most important chapter in this book.

FOURTH, since content is not visible on the internet without SEO, I had to include a strategy on how to make your content rank high in search engines – since most of website traffic comes from search engines. Therefore, I put SEO and Inbound Marketing as the fourth chapter.

FIFTH, is Online Marketing although most chapters are branches from online marketing, I put this as a separate chapter because of the generality of the points it had. It's an extremely important chapter and involves knowledge for the online world of marketing.

SIXTH, is Social Media Marketing due to its importance in this digitally social age.

SEVENTH, I put Email Marketing since all the previous chapters lead towards building an email list and acquiring customers, I figured this chapter comes after them... since you won't send any emails if you don't have an email list, right?

EIGHTH, Word-of-Mouth Marketing or commonly known as Referral Marketing. The way to make people promote your business for free... the most important chapter after direct-response and content marketing (in my opinion). However, without completing the previous chapters – this becomes useless.

NINTH, Influencer Marketing. The way to make influential people promote your business or product... a real game changer. But, since influencers don't just promote any crap, it will be better if you've mastered the previous chapters. (I know many people will skip to this chapter first... let's see if you're undisciplined like them).

TENTH, Mistakes from 23 Entrepreneurs, the place where all the influencers share their biggest mistakes.

Then I ended with final notes and my contact details in case you have any questions (make sure you write down any questions you have along the way).

I recommend you follow the book in the way it is organized.

IMPORTANT: There are 94 mistakes in this book and each one ends with an "Action Plan". These are actions you must take throughout the book. This isn't a theory book you just read and throw away. So please, ensure you go through the Action Plans.

Also, under each Action Plan, I included something I called an "Undefeated Marketing Secret". There are 94 of them and I put them in a checklist (available in the bonus material). I did this so you can refer to the advice quickly from just a sheet of paper rather than flicking through the book pages one by one. Think of them as the 94 codes an Undefeated Marketer should live by.

I've made this book very easy to follow and remember. You have no excuses for not taking action!

1
GENERAL MARKETING

Just general common mistakes made by entrepreneurs that you should avoid to build a strong foundation.

1. Selling What No One Wants

Has anyone bought what you're selling? Or did you just get a lot of friends and family telling you "yes"? Did you even try selling it or getting feedback?

If people have already bought what you're selling (or from a competitor who sells the same), then you can afford to invest marketing efforts into it. Otherwise, it would be just a waste of time. Because if no one wants it in the first place, then you could do all the marketing there is and nothing would work. Even if you do manage to sell it using all the emotional sales techniques there is, the number of unhappy customers that would send you hate mails online would be enough to force you out of business the next day... assuming the product is bad or useless.

When entrepreneurs ask for feedback, a lot of them ask, "Do you like the idea of our product?", "Would you buy our product?" – But what most entrepreneurs don't realize is, most people you interview for feedback who say "yes" actually mean "yes, it would be a good idea but for someone else. Not me." – That's because when you ask people for feedback, they switch onto "advisor mode" and answer your questions by giving you advise on what they perceive people would like or do. For that reason, you should always ask for a sale for those that do say "yes", to find out if they really mean "yes, I would buy it" or "yes, but not for me."

Action Plan

Select a group of people (around 100) to interview and authenticate your answers by taking pre-orders on your product even if it's not been manufactured yet... just like crowd funding. You can always refund the money back to the customer if anything goes wrong... as long as you don't spend it.

> **Undefeated Marketing Secret #1: Sell Things in High Demand**

2.   Selling Just to Make Money

Are you in it for the money or because you love it? For me, it's both, I love building things from scratch and I happen to be those people who love to learn almost every field of study there is. From alternative medicine to mechanical engineering to farming – the whole lot. So, I am naturally passionate about a lot of things – however, marketing is my ultimate passion because from marketing, I can sell whatever I want. In fact, the whole business world is built around selling and we can't live without it. Everyone needs to know marketing and sales.

So back to the topic... I know many people who are in it just for the money, only the money, nothing more! Entrepreneurs who are only in it for the money give up easily when things don't go as planned, and let me tell you something, not everything goes as planned! There are many uncertainties in building a company, so acknowledging this fact and preparing yourself for the bad days is the one thing every entrepreneur should do – the same way we put fire extinguishers and first-aid kits all over the work place, you should have emergency funds and back up plans for your startups.

Whether you're passionate for a lot of things or just one, the most important thing is to have focus on one goal until success.

If you bought this book because you have some products or a startup idea you wanted to sell for a quick buck, then don't despair – you can still create an artificial-like passion or enthusiasm. I'll tell you how to achieve that in just a bit. First, I need to address two important things...

Some people 'do' build companies with no passion other than their passion to make money – but in order to build something great and world changing, you NEED passion. Imagine if Mark Zuckerberg had no passion for Facebook and just sold it off to Yahoo for $1 billion, where would Facebook be right now and what would Mark's net worth be?

The other thing is, the advice of "follow your passion and money will follow" is a load of crap. If the thing you are passionate about has no demand in the market, then pursuing it as a business is a waste of time… it's a hobby. Even if 100 people told you that they like your idea, their feedback means nothing unless they gave you money for pre-orders – it's no wonder people validate their ideas through crowd funding.

When I say you need passion, I mean you'll do anything and everything to make it a reality and never give up.

Okay!

PURPOSE

So, if you have no passion or motivation in what you're doing, you need to think of a bigger purpose of why you're doing it. Let's say you only want to sell Argan oil online because someone told you about its high demand. Think of why you want that money, will you use it to help poor people? Will you use it to fund an idea, which you are passionate about?

If you've lost passion in what you're doing, then stop for a moment and remember why you started in the first place. As humans, we get tangled up with present circumstances so much that we forget why we started in the first place.

SKILL

I am a graduate of civil engineering and I loved studying it, until I didn't. It all disappeared in my second and third year when I had to do these complicated calculations – because I didn't know how to do them, I hated them. But in my first year, I loved it – because I was good at it. When you're good at something, you will enjoy it!

ENERGY

Sometimes, it's just a problem with your energy levels. Nothing makes you tick. You drag yourself through every part of life including work.

Action Plan

Get a pen and paper, and write down your purpose for doing it. Think of it as your mission rather than just a passion or a hobby. Put that piece of paper at your working place so you can remind yourself of your mission when you're not feeling so energetic.

Know your strengths and weaknesses and work on enhancing your skills. For example, if you are good at writing, then take the time to learn everything about writing until you master your skill. You can try to mix two skills together like, nutrition and graphic design to create nutrition related info graphics etc. Work on what you are good at, until you become an expert at it... you'll enjoy it then.

Go to sleep, have a nap, eat well, go to the doctor – these could all solve your problems for low energy. On the other hand, there could be an annoying thing in your life that's sucking all the energy out of you.... Such as a job you hate or someone who's making your life a living hell. Get rid of it!

Final Note: To put everything in just a few words, if you have a mission, skill and energy, you're good to go. Remember that there are two types of businesses;

a)   Business you build around a passion
b)   Passion you build around a business

Which one is better? Whatever is in more demand!

(Go and download "The Commitment Pledge" from the bonus material, sign it and put it on your desk)

Undefeated Marketing Secret #2: Your passion for something is your ability to work the hardest and never give up on it.

---

3.   Think You Need a Huge Budget

So, you're passionate and you've established demand for your product. You have competitors and they have much more marketing dollars than you can ever dream of making in a lifetime. You'll never win with a few hundred or thousand bucks against their billion dollar marketing budgets.

That's what they want you to believe so to scare you away. Wanna know the good news? It's not true and it doesn't matter anyway. That advice is just too old. With technology, you can now outsource everything overseas for just a fraction of what they pay. You can reach over a billion people just through the internet. Today, people are connected more than ever. That's why I say, "It doesn't matter!"

Because while Starbucks hires in-house social media marketing employees for $40,000 a year, you can outsource the work for $250 - $500 a month. Don't forget that big companies hire big teams, so that $40,000 adds up to hit millions.

Then comes the website... large companies pay ten and hundred thousand dollar range for websites... you can get a professional website for around $2,000... sometimes, much less.

The point is; you can compete with a million dollar budget easily if you use your resources effectively.

Perhaps, hiring overseas workers are cheap because they're just bad at what they do and big companies hire talented people. You are right, sometimes, you'll hire someone for cheap and they return bad work – I've experienced the same. But, this isn't the result of bad employees; it's the result of bad hiring.

Let's face it; large companies can also hire crappy employees and they do. Not everyone that passes the interview process turns out to be a successful employee. You'll just have to take your chances.

There are people who do excellent work at cheap prices and this happens for two main reasons, one, they undervalue their worth. Two, they live in a country where labor is so cheap, a $1,000 salary lasts them for months.

Here's a tip for hiring overseas workers, always hire them like you would hire an in-house employee and that includes running them through the tough hiring process every other employee goes through. Make sure you establish clear expectations and communicate regularly with them... and of course, don't forget skill.

I'm not against hiring in-house, in fact, I prefer in-house but if you have limited resources, you need to find a way around it. And the best way is to hire overseas workers.

Second thing is, huge marketing budgets include meaningless TV commercials, billboards and all the other crappy methods of non-direct response advertising that produce no measurable results. It's one of the reasons large companies have great budgets, because they waste it on non-direct response advertising.

Non-direct response advertising is when an advertisement has no call to action in the end just like most billboards and TV commercials; they just create awareness with something memorable. They don't ask you to buy on the spot.

On the other hand, you have direct-response advertising which demands action from people at the end and offers measurable results (since most of the time you will attach a coupon with a code at the bottom of an advertisement that the prospect will have to hand out to receive the offer). Not only is direct-response advertising measurable but (in most cases), it also converts better. More people will respond to a direct-response AD that tells them what to do, than a non-direct response AD that leaves them confused.

So, when I say, their budgets don't matter – trust me... they really don't matter as much as people make it seem. The differences are insignificant and most importantly, they do not result in you failing. Being small also has an advantage – you are able to respond to real-time feedback compared to large companies that need to go through levels of bureaucracy and a hierarchy of people to just arrive at a decision. They are slow and speed matters in businesses.

Action Plan

Hire cheap overseas freelancers to do your work and ensure you hire skillful people. Take time to find out bargains instead of paying the highest possible price like many businesses do. Remember that higher budgets do not mean better results. A million dollar team in the U.S, can cost a few thousand dollars overseas. (I have included a list of websites to find cheap talent in the bonuses).

Make sure you also use marketing strategies that are measurable rather than throwing your money on unmeasurable promotions.

> *Undefeated Marketing Secret #3: Don't be intimidated by large marketing budgets, you can get near equivalent work done with a fraction of what they pay.*

4. Not Marketing Because of Cost (Instead of ROI)

"Marketing is expensive! It costs so much".
That's what beginners say. They waste their money to add unimportant features to a product and leave nothing to

promote. They think that if they build it, customers will come. But customers don't come when you build it; they come when you promote it and tell them about it. Without marketing, you just have a product hidden in the basement…no one will know about it to actually buy it.

Marketing is never expensive as long as you get a return on investment (ROI), then that's all that matters. If you spend $200 on Facebook AD that gets you $400, then Facebook ADs are not expensive and are worth the investment.

Likewise, if you invest $1billion dollars and get $2billion in return, then that wasn't expensive either. But, let's stick to the $200 example for now, shall we?

Action Plan

Treat all your marketing costs based on how much money they can make you and not how much their initial cost is. Test with the minimum amount possible to test each marketing strategy and identify the ones that offer the highest returns. Once you find out the most profitable marketing strategy, then do more of it. I would say, test with $50 and see what happens if you're running online Pay Per Click (PPC) ADs.

> *Undefeated Marketing Secret #4: Marketing is only expensive if it has a negative ROI.*

5.   Ignoring Competition

There are entrepreneurs that are scared of competitors and then there are those who ignore them totally, as if they don't exist. Both are wrong!

Being scared just holds you back from taking action and ignoring them ignores the fact that they still exist and they still compete to steal customers from you. Competitors are called competitors because they serve something similar to you to your target customers. They compete to close more sales than you.

You should never ever ignore them. Always be aware of what they are doing. On the other hand, don't let watching them consume your time.

Action Plan

Have your competitors in peripheral vision. But, have your main focus on pleasing the customer and offering them the best of service.

Undefeated Marketing Secret #5: Ignoring the competition is a great way to get an unexpected knockout punch – and watching them is a great way to lose focus.

---

6.   Having no Position in The Market

How do two different competitors thrive while offering similar products? Is it just random?

Of course not. It's all about positioning. But, what is positioning? It is when you differentiate yourself from the competition in the consumers mind. In my opinion, positioning is the most important part in marketing. Without positioning, you are just another choice for the consumer and there is nothing special about you other than your cheap prices and convenient distance.

In order to succeed in a crowded market, you need to stand out. When you stand out, you become THE choice rather than just another choice.

It doesn't matter how boring your product seems, you can always stand out with it. There are many ways to make yourself unique even if your product seems boring.

Look at WalMart and Costco for example, they are both successful retailers and they sell similar groceries and stuff. Yet, they are both unique. One is the lowest price leader and the other is a membership-only warehouse that sells in bulk. That difference is what gives them different positions in our minds, because if they didn't do that, they would be just another local retailer. (I have included a positioning formula that Amazon.com uses in the bonus material).

Most businesses don't take positioning seriously (or don't know what it is) and therefore, people don't take them seriously. These businesses offer nothing different from the rest and so customers treat them the same and go to them only based on convenience (price & distance).

Al Ries, author of "Positioning: The Battle for Your Mind", says that positioning is the single word that comes to mind when a brand's name is mentioned.

To stand out, you need to have a Unique Selling Proposition (USP) based on any of the following:
*   Price – not recommended

- Product
- Place
- Color
- Size
- Scent
- Celebrity endorsement
- Location
- Hours of operation
- Delivery Style
- Being number #1
- Much more

(I have included these in the bonuses for you to print)

You need to ensure that the customer benefits from your USP – something that really matters to them.

You will then use the USP to incorporate into your positioning statement.

Just to let you know, there's a lot of marketers that say USP and positioning is the same thing... but USP is just a benefit that your product has... sometimes, your USP will be part of your positioning, sometimes, it won't... it just depends.

Action Plan

Step 1: Make a list of all competitors that offer similar products/services – the bigger the list, the better.

Step 2: Visit your competitor's websites.

Step 3: From the first website, write down each promise, benefit and statement they make. If you find the same statement from other websites, then just draw a line next to it and keep stick counting the number of times it appears.

Step 4: Repeat for the rest of your list.

When you're done, you'll find out that everyone says just about the same thing – and that's good news for you. Now, it's time for you to figure out a way to be different so you can dominate your market.

Step 5: Answer your customer's question to come up with a USP:

Why should I choose you over everyone else?

(I have included a worksheet for all these steps (USP, Positioning Formula and Competitor Research List) in the bonuses, so go and download them)

> *Undefeated Marketing Secret #6: Make competition irrelevant by being unique and different so you can dominate a special place in the customers mind.*

7.   Not Knowing Your Ideal Customer

Do you know who you're selling to? Whom does your product or service appeal to? What kinds of people buy from you the most?

This question goes hand in hand with the previous part on USP's. You can't develop a USP if you don't know who your offer is for in the first place.

A lot of businesses just want to sell to everyone. I don't blame them, who wouldn't want everyone to buy from them? I'd love it! But, unfortunately, you can't impress everyone and as the saying goes "If you market to everyone, you market to no one." That's because when you say, "Hey everybody", it doesn't feel intimate compared to saying, "Hey broke entrepreneur" or "Hey college student" or whatever the person's problem is.

If you're selling golf carts, you'd most likely target 45+ year old men that earn an income of $70K + a year, not very tech savvy and regularly hang out with "the boys" every weekend for a few rounds of golf – this is known as the buyer persona.

Then you can take it up another notch by splitting up your buyer persona into three groups… your must-buy-now buyer, your can-buy-now buyers and ordinary buyers. All these three types of buyers match your buyer persona, but they have a little difference.

Your must-buy-now buyers are those that have had a sudden change in their lives or want a sudden change in their lives that they "need" your product RIGHT NOW! You can-buy-now buyers are rich or people with enough money to buy your product or service but don't need it now; however, you could nudge them to take action if you infuse a sense of urgency. The ordinary buyer is a person who sort of matches your buyer persona – he may or may not buy from you.

The reason you split them up into three groups is because you want to identify the easiest and hungriest prospects that need to buy now.

If you sell beds, then a must-now-buyer would be someone who is moving or just moved to a new home. A can-now-buyer would be someone who just had a new baby or been promoted at their job. Your ordinary buyer would just be a homeowner.

So who should you focus on?
•   Must-Now Buyer – Cheapest and Easiest
•   Can-Now Buyer – Medium
•   Ordinary Buyer – Expensive and Unsure
The answer is the first two… for now.

Action Plan

Step 1: Find out to whom your product appeals to, who needs it, who uses it and who would buy it to create your buyers persona. (I've included a quick and easy guide in the bonuses).

Step 2: Find out the characteristics of a must-buy-now and a can-buy-now buyer within your marketplace. For example, do they need to move houses? Or give birth to a baby? – What other sudden event in their lives makes them a must or can-buy now buyer?

> *Undefeated Marketing Secret #7: Know your target audience before shooting at them with sales letters; aim before you shoot.*

8. Talking About Yourself

Me, Me, Me. That's how most business promotions sound like today. All they ever talk about is their brand, their products and how great they are.

And yes, you probably are an awesome brand with outstanding products and an interesting background, but no one likes a person or business that just talks about themselves – people want to talk too. People want you to communicate their problems, desires and interests. They want a brand that understands them, just like a close, helpful friend.

And just like a close, helpful friend, if you care about them, they will care about you, and if they care about you, you get the sale.

You shouldn't sell all the time. Don't be afraid to give. When you consistently give people a lot of value, people will want to pay you back by buying from you.

I remember the last time I gave this advice on Instagram, someone commented, "business is business". He is right, but I'm not telling you to give away expensive things for free. I'm telling you to offer free advice, help, a thank you card, small gifts... and to stop ending everything with a sale.

THEN, after like 6 times, 10 times, 20 times, you can ask for a sale. You'll be surprised how much sales you will make when you help more and ask less.

Action Plan

Step 1: Find out what keeps your customers up at night, what do they care about?

Step 2: Talk to them about it and become their closest friend.

Step 3: Don't ask them to buy after each conversation, letter and email.

Step 4: Just talk to them like a friend – it's not rocket science.

> *Undefeated Marketing Secret #8: Don't talk about yourself all the time; keep it minimal and give more.*

9.   Not Building Pre-Launch Hype

I've been there and probably you have too.

You work really hard on a product, create social media accounts and on launch day, you announce the news: "WE ARE LIVE"… the only problem is, you've only got grandma and close cousins on social media and email list. You launched a product to no one, now you have to search for customers and that takes time.

You could have avoided it if you started promoting it earlier… or as we like to say, create a prelaunch hype.

You don't create a website and social media account a week before – you start building hype 6 months to a year before your launch date. Build an audience and then sell to them. Get people excited about your new business – the minimum should be at least, 3 months.

Have you ever seen those "coming soon" pages on websites that collect people's emails in exchange for being the "first to know" about their startup? Well, that's what you should do as well.

This is a great time to communicate with people without selling, just like we mentioned before – now is the chance to build a new group of friends for your business.

Action Plan

Create social media accounts, a coming-soon page on your website collecting people's emails (use MailChimp, it's free for the first 2,000 email subscribers and you can then export those contacts to a better service such as Aweber, GetResponse or Infusionsoft once you launch).

Step 1: Buy a ".com" domain name from namescheap.com (but read step 2, before you do this).

Step 2: Purchase hosting – siteground.com is the best hosting service because of their 24/7 support, powerful machines and a lot of other stuff – but it's up to you. If you do decide to go for Siteground.com however, then I recommend you start with their "StartUp shared hosting" plan. Here's something else; Siteground.com offers a free domain name with every purchase – so you can get 2 in 1 if you choose to host with siteground.com. Did I also mention they are affordable?

Step 3: Set up a free wordpress.org site (not wordpress.com) and host it with your hosting provider. (Wordpress is used by over 74.6 million sites). [1]

Step 4: Download a free Wordpress theme such as launcheffectapp.com to create your coming-soon page.

Step 5: Create a free MailChimp account and Integrate MailChimp with the opt in box so the emails get saved onto MailChimp (or any other email marketing service you're using).

Step 6: Build your email list with guest blogging and all the other stuff you'll learn through this book.

> **Undefeated Marketing Secret #9: Build hype for your product months before the launch date.**

10. Selling Before Establishing Credibility and Trust

Has a stranger ever walked up to you trying to sell you something? Did you buy what he/she sold?

You probably ignored them or just said "no, thanks" and kept walking. If you did buy however, it was probably because they told you what company they worked for, what they did and whatever else to build trust with you. Or, the person was intimidating so you just bought out of fear.

Whatever the case is, I know it and you know it – no one buys from someone they don't trust.

You would never buy an iPhone from a stranger walking on the street even if it was new and cheaper than the one from the store. You'd buy it from the store even if it's more expensive, that's because you trust a brick and mortar establishment and not the stranger selling on foot.

Here's 6 ways to create credibility for your business/self:

- Testimonials
- Research and reports (citing from reputable magazines, experts, universities etc.)
- Personal Profiles of the team and experts behind the product/startup/whatever
- Photographs of before and after results or how the product is made
- Celebrity endorsement
- Degrees, certifications and awards

But then, there's another problem…

Credibility isn't enough; you need something else to strengthen it. Imagine you went to buy a car and the salesman tells you how awesome the car is. How many seats it has. How it goes from 0 to 60mph in 5 seconds. How it's been rated 5 stars for safety and all the other promises a car salesman will make.

If you're like most people, you wouldn't believe what he just said. That's because all he's done is make claims and promises, but hasn't proven any of it to you.

For proof, the salesman shows you a track record. He shows you the number of satisfied customers in the past.

For a fitness product, you'd show how many people lost weight and/or gained muscle.

For an education product, you'd show the number of people that graduated and had success with what they learnt.

Track record can be in the form of testimonials, case studies, statistical data etc.

Don't mix up credibility and track record – they are both needed to build trust.

Credibility tells the customer that you, your firm or establishment is trustworthy and worth dealing/working with – that you're not a thief.

Track record shows that what you're selling really works. Instead of telling the customer what to think, you show him hard evidence that he will consider and make a decision from.

With the skeptic customers of these days, you need both – no matter how similar they sound.

Action Plan

Apply at least one of the methods mentioned above to establish credibility. Then apply one method to show track record – then work your way up and add more as time passes. The more testimonials, endorsements etc. you have, the better. (I've included a table with methods for establishing credibility and track record in the bonus material).

If you've never had any customers, then give away a few samples to prospects. In fact, you should have sold a few when you were interviewing potential customers while validating your idea. Either way, just get someone to use your product and tell you their story and experience with the product and how it changed their life. Even the most boring product can be life changing – like a toothbrush… giving you sparkling clean teeth that amazed the dentist, etc…

Undefeated Marketing Secret #10: People buy from credible businesses with a track record.

---

11. Afraid of Wasting Time Planning

There are two main benefits of planning.

One, it gets rid of procrastination because you'll feel obligated to follow the plan you spent time to create.

Two, you will save time, because instead of constantly thinking of what you should do, you'll just be executing your step-by-step plan.

In other words, planning is a time saver and a procrastination killer (there is actually more than two, but I believe these matter the most).

Experts such as Brian Tracy, says that planning 10-12 minutes a day, can save you up to two hours daily.[2] Another info graphic from the Huffington Post shows that you could possibly waste 3 hours + $50 a week, just on meals if you don't plan (this isn't business. This is just food).[3]

I could go on and on about the benefits of planning, but you get the point.

Action Plan

Plan and schedule everything you do on a calendar.

You can download the Wordpress Editorial Calendar Plugin at https://wordpress.org/plugins/editorial-calendar/

Or you can download the editorial calendar by HubSpot at http://offers.hubspot.com/blog-editorial-calendar In fact, I highly recommend it!

I personally use Google Calendar for my regular daily life – If you're a one-man business, you can also plan content directly on the calendar too.

Whatever you decide to do – just ensure you schedule it on some sort of calendar.

> **Undefeated Marketing Secret #11: Plan before you execute – or waste time and fall behind.**

12. Ignoring Old Customers

I know it's tempting to acquire new customers all the time... and you should, but not at the expense of your current customers. The ones that bought from you when you had only a small number or no customers at all... the early adopters. Many businesses hire the best talent to acquire new customers and scrappy stuff to current customers.

People that bought from you in the past are more likely to buy from you in the future (if they were satisfied). When you invest marketing dollars on a current customer, you get a higher chance of action (because they've broken the ice with you already). On the other hand, when you invest marketing dollars on potential (cold) prospects who don't know you already, your response rate will be low and the costs will be high.

It's better to sell several products to several thousand customers than one product to millions – of course, this isn't to say that you shouldn't acquire new customers, just don't do it at the expense of ignoring your old ones.

It's best to create products at different values. Like the figure below:

This is known as the value ladder. You have products at different values along with a subscription plan for continuous income. As you can see from the figure, you start out with a free bait to capture leads (potential customers), then you move up with products sold at a higher price until you reach your best product. The subscription plan is where you bill a customer every week or month and offer consistent value in return – this is the constant source of oxygen to your businesses – don't ignore it.

So what could your value ladder look like if you were in the information selling business?

- Bait: Free eBook, video, email course etc.
- Front End: Free book, lectures on DVD (pay shipping only)
- Middle: Course for beginners $300 - $1,000
- Front End: Consulting / Advanced Course $1,500 +
- Subscription plan: Insider newsletter, membership for an expert group, etc.
- What would a value ladder look like if you were an ecommerce startup?
- Bait: Free eBook, video, email course, discount coupon etc.
- Front End: Free product (pay shipping only)
- Middle: Product in the $100 – 300 range
- Front End: Best product

Subscription plan: Membership for exclusive discounts, fast shipping, etc. (think Amazon Prime).

Of course, my examples were just examples, not what you should do. You know your business and customer better than me.

Another thing to point out is, don't limit your value ladder to just 4 stages like in the above examples. The more products you have, the more you can offer your customers and the more each customer will be worth. The more valuable they are, the more you can spend to acquire them.

Action Plan

Give more time to your old customers and look for more ways to help them – produce more products that will help them even more.

> **Undefeated Marketing Secret #12: Create more products for current customers.**

13. Trying to Please Everyone

You can't please everyone. I can't please everyone. No one can please everyone.

So don't try to.

So who should you please?

Well... your paying customers... the majority of them... the best ones.

The last thing you want to do is please someone who isn't even your customer in the first place. You'll have haters on social media, your blog and your email list. If their feedback is meaningful and sounds like a good idea, then sure, you can try it out. But, if it's just hate mail, throw it away.

Here's a story that you'll hear or have probably already heard a lot...

When Malcolm Gladwell used to oversimplify scientific research in his books, scientists would critic him because they were too simple.

So Gladwell said, "If my books appear to a reader to be oversimplified, then you shouldn't read them: You're not the audience."

That's exactly it! Gladwell doesn't write for scientists, he writes for regular people.

Gladwell doesn't try to impress scientists, he impresses his audience. You should do the same in your business. Impress your customers and ignore non-customers.

Action Plan

Use your judgment in determining what feedback you should take and which you shouldn't. Remember that the most valuable feedback comes from paying customers that have used your products.

> **Undefeated Marketing Secret #13: You can't impress everyone, so don't try to.**

14. You're Confusing

If you're selling a valuable product, then sell it in luxury/valuable packaging. If you sell fresh vegetables, then don't put them in a plastic box, lay them down separately so the customer can make their choice.. If you offer expensive food at your restaurant, don't just wrap it in a takeaway paper bag; put it in a luxurious looking box. Don't confuse the customer by claiming one thing and then presenting it in a totally different way. Many entrepreneurs spend so much time on making the product so good, they forget about presentation.

Maybe it's because you believe in "Don't judge a book by its cover" or you're just being lazy and cheap about it.

Whatever the reason is... presentation is just as important as the product itself.

People DO judge a book by its cover and marketers know that – and as a marketer, you should remember this point too – it's all about the cover!

Action Plan

Present your product exactly as you'd like the customer to see it. For example, luxury product = valuable luxury packaging, creative product = creative/fun packaging, fresh product = natural fresh presentation, etc. This applies to your website too!

> **Undefeated Marketing Secret #14: People judge a book by its cover – so sell them the cover.**

15. Ignoring Snail Mail because it's Too Old School

Before you call me old school, let me ask you a question... Do you prefer a physical thank you card or an electronic version of it?

If you're like most people, you'd prefer the physical card because it's something you can put on your desk rather than lose in your inbox along with the junk mail.

Regardless of how techy people are becoming, the majority still prefer print. But, let's say that changes in the future; let's just assume people will prefer electronic over print in the near future.

If that happens, your inbox will be flooded with junk mail and newsletters from businesses.

However, your home mailbox will be almost empty – because as we advance in technology, businesses are moving with us too and starting to leave traditional methods behind, which is good. Don't get me wrong, your business must move with technology.

The only problem here is, as a business, your email will have to compete with the other 50 or 100 daily promotions your customers get and that's really not good for your email open rates.

Let me put it this way…

Why fight for a crowded inbox, when you can quietly land in their empty mailbox?

Instead of copying all the 1,000,000,000,000 businesses that land the spam folder – why don't you stand out and send your mail through their mailbox. Not only will you stand out, but you'll also get their full attention. Even if they don't have time to read it, they'll probably leave it on the table and read it later. But, when it's an email left for later, that little poor thing sinks to the 5th page in a few hours and the person forgets to read it.

That's not all… it gets better…

With direct mail, you don't need people to subscribe to your mailing list – because you can rent existing lists.

It's one of the fastest ways to grow a business.

Rent a mailing list, hire an awesome copywriter (or write it yourself if you're a great copywriter) and send the promotion to targeted prospects from that list.

It's a very effective way to grow your business from just a few thousand dollars.

I understand that email is almost free to send, but for those of you who want a rapid growth, I suggest you follow this method. It is well worth the investment if you have a good product, killer copy and an irresistible offer with a guarantee at the end, you could make a killing.

Companies such as The Wall Street Journal and American Express have made billions of dollars in revenue through direct order mail – and it can cost just as low as a grocery clerk's monthly salary. If you don't even have that much, then give it a run after you've made a few thousand dollars online.

Action Plan

Rent a mailing list and send physical direct mail to their mailbox – don't forget to have killer copy (you should hire a copywriter if you don't know how to write sales letters). You can hire a copywriter if you need to, but make sure they have a successful track record and written a few "controls".

Undefeated Marketing Secret #15: Use snail mail. Don't follow the crowd – be unique.

---

16. Doing Everything Alone and Being Greedy With Partners

It's common sense… two active people can achieve more than one active person. How about one person with customers and one person with a product – how does that sound? Seems like one can't do without the other. In that case, partnership would be the best thing you can do.

Entrepreneurs do partner up with others – no problem there.

The problem arises when splitting the returns. Entrepreneurs start to get cheap and greedy. But, forget about how much your partner takes and look at it this way...

How much would it cost you to acquire the customers on your own? Would it cost more or less?

If partnering up is cheaper and profitable, then by all means, go for it. What if it costs a bit more but it's still profitable? Should you still partner up? Of course! There's nothing better than instant access to another businesses customers – it saves time and the hassle.

What kind of businesses do you partner up with?

Ideally, you would partner up with non-competing businesses that is related to yours. For example, if you're a protein bar company, you'd partner up with a gym. If you're an author, you'd partner up with a blogger with a large reader base.

You sometimes can partner up with a competitor, but this is only in rare cases. Such as a blogger with a blogger. An author and another author etc.

Action Plan

Partner up with businesses that are related to you and don't be cheap about it.

> *Undefeated Marketing Secret #16: Don't be cheap with partners – they give you easy access to customers – so be grateful.*

17. Afraid of Big Competitors

Ever heard of the 80/20 rule? Quick frankly, I've gotten sick of it! But, it is almost true – 20% of things give 80% of the results and vice versa.

So why am I telling you this?

Well, you know your big competitors? How many customers do they have? 100,000? 250,000 maybe? Whatever it is, it's only 20% of their customers that create 80% of their sales. The other 80%? Well... they only make around 20% of sales.

20% of 100,000 customers = 20,000 customers

20% of 250,000 customers = 50,000 customers

Now, I don't know what business you're in, but for online startups.... Guest blogging and other marketing strategies... you could surpass those numbers. Heck, some people have gotten 100,000 subscribers in a year, others have done that in a week![4] (You can read about that here:

http://fourhourworkweek.com/2014/07/21/harrys-prelaunchr-email)

But, there's even better news. You don't need to have the same amount of customers to make more money than your competitors. Remember the value ladder I talked about earlier? Do your competitors have one of those? If they do not, you already have an advantage. If they do? Make a deeper one and you can bring out more value per customer than your competitors ever will.

Even better, remember the USP and positioning we talked about earlier too? That will make you stand out – and if you position yourself as a premium product/service business, you can charge more than your competitors – that's a double win.

All the stuff you've learnt up until now is just the start, and already you have enough knowledge to knockout most competitors.

If you've read the post on how Harry's managed to get 100,000 subscribers in a week and you replicate their strategy for your startup, your competitors will get agitated. Of course, you may not be able to get 100,000 in a week like they did, but you'd have a chance to grow faster than the majority – or you may get over 100,000 – you'll never know, you'll have to try it out.

Action Plan

Don't let big companies intimidate you and make you feel like you don't stand a chance. If you psychologically believe it's impossible, then you've already lost.

Undefeated Marketing Secret #17: Don't be intimidated by large companies – they are smaller than you think.

2
CONVERSION MARKETING

This chapter is about website conversions. I put it here because usually, businesses set up their websites right after they've got the basics figured out. Traffic is worthless if you don't convert it. Mistakes made in this field will lower your conversion rates.

18. Giving a Web Design Project to a Web Designer

Pretty ironic huh?

Who's gonna design your website then? And what does a web designer do?

Let me first start by mentioning the difference between a web developer and a web designer for those who don't know.

A web developer is the person that builds the websites functionality – he's the builder.

A web designer is the person that creates the aesthetics and the appearance – he's the architect/ exterior designer.

A lot of people mix up the two and call them both web developers – maybe that's because a website needs both web development and design to be created – so people just call it web development.

So, here's the problem;

Most web designers don't know marketing and so they focus only on how good the website looks – which is good for conversions, but it's not good enough.

When you create a business website, your website isn't there just to make you look good – it's a marketing tool – in fact, it's one of the best tools to build your email list with.

Since it's a marketing tool, you need an online marketer to design it. Whether the online marketer knows web design or works with a web designer, that's up to you to decide.

Marketers test and tweak their websites all the time to see which designs and copy converts more visitors into email subscribers/customers.

Your website isn't there just to make you look good and professional. It's there to convert traffic into leads – because without leads, your business will die... so please, take this seriously.

Here's a tip: Go for a paid theme which is compatible with wordpress.org, mobile friendly and search engine optimized. To save you time searching for such a theme, just go to studiopress.com – then your developer can build your website from there. They also have their own recommended developers who are familiar with the framework, here at: http://www.studiopress.com/genesis-developers/

Action Plan

Hire a web developer with marketing knowledge or a team of developers and marketers that work together.

> *Undefeated Marketing Secret #18: Websites are marketing tools – let marketers build them.*

19. Having no Blog

Whether you're an online cookie startup, a tech company or a brick and mortar company – you NEED a blog.

Your blog is what attracts leads, establishes your expertise, offers self-help to people, increases your online exposure, and everything else that's good for your company.

A study by HubSpot found that companies who blog are 13x more likely to get a positive marketing ROI.[5]

A lot of traffic comes from search engines. But, what do people usually search for?

HELP. They search for solutions to the problems they have. They ask questions to find a solution for their problems. The results they get will be a bunch of blog posts.

So, if you don't have a blog – you're losing out on a load of traffic.

Action Plan

Include a blog on your company's website.

> *Undefeated Marketing Secret #19: A company blog is the best tool to attract and educate potential customers.*

20. Afraid of Opt-in Forms on Site

Opt-in forms, especially pop-ups have a bad reputation. They are annoying, they distract visitors and they make your website feel kind of "salesy".

It's all true. But, you want to know what they also do? THEY BUILD YOUR EMAIL LIST. Frankly, that's all that matters. Regardless of how insensitive and selfish that sounds, you need to sacrifice a bit of the user experience in exchange for acquiring leads. YOU NEED LEADS. So, you have no other choice.

Here's a list of nine popular types of opt-in forms:

1. Pop-ups – The thing that jumps right into your face.

2. Content upgrades – The little download links inside the content

⭐ Want to know which email subject I've used to get Rand's attention? :)
Click here and I will email it to you!

3. Side bar opt-in – The traditional ones in the sidebar

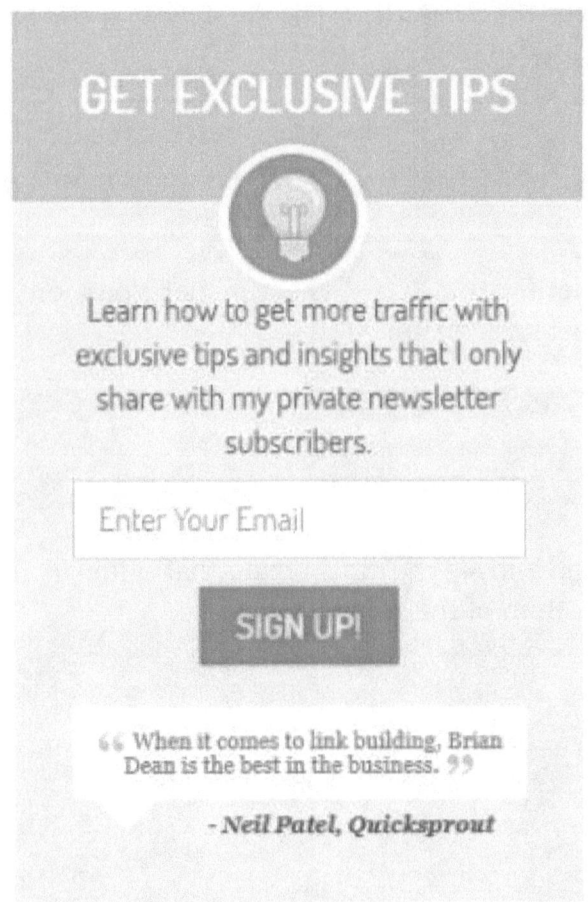

4. Feature box – That big box on top of the site but under the menu.

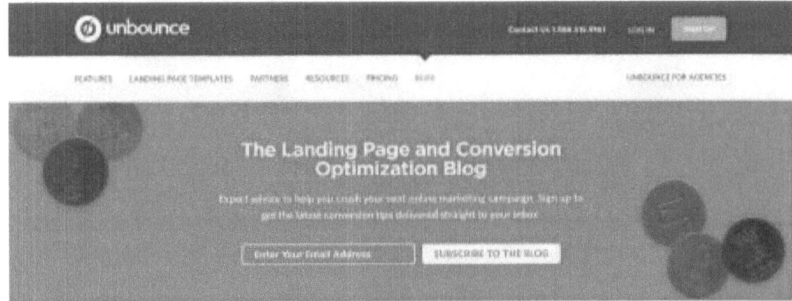

5.   After post opt-in – The small box at the bottom of an article

6.   Notification bar – The bar that floats on top of a websites menu.

7.   Slide in – The tiny boxes that slide in from the bottom of the screen.

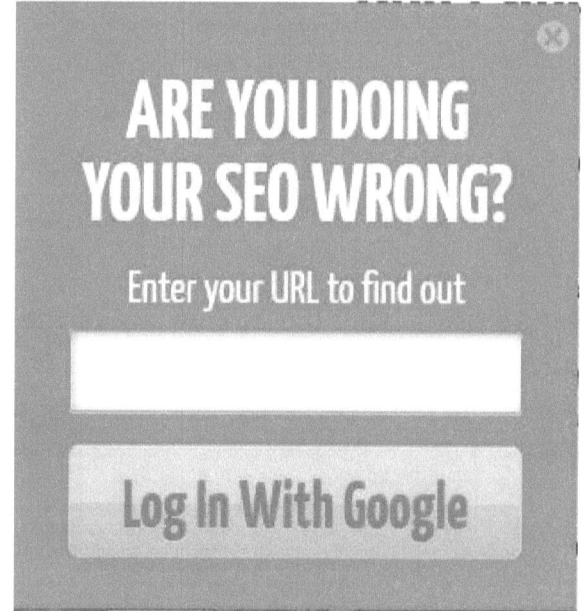

8.   Landing page – The stand-alone page that has only one objective… get emails.

9.   Full screen opt-in – The huge box that covers the entire website.

Obviously, you don't need to use all of them – in fact, you shouldn't. Having 9 different opt-in forms all over your website is just crazy.

Every website is different, so there is a bit of flexibility in terms of what opt-in forms you use. However, here are some things you need to know;

- Sidebars on the left hand side convert better: According to a research study conducted by Nielsen Norman Group[6], people look more on the left side than the right side. (Make sure you check out the research).
- Feature boxes have one of the highest conversion rates.
- After post opt-ins are great because they are at the end of each article. If people read all the way to the end, they're likely to want more by subscribing to your list – so it's a great place to have one.
- People love going to the "About" page so ensure you put several opt-in boxes throughout the page – it's one of the highest visited pages.
- Content Upgrades are the BEST and a MUST have. When someone reads an article on your blog, they read it because it solves a problem or fulfills a

burning desire. But, you can't just add every single piece of info on an article – so you create an exclusive bonus that compliments the article they are already reading... also known as content upgrades. These things have an extremely high conversion rate, ignoring them is a serious mistake!

Action Plan

Step 1: Put a feature box on the top of your website.

Step 2: Put your sidebar on the left (if you use Wordpress, the Studiopress themes allow you to easily move the sidebar to the left side without code. The support team will assist you if you have a problem).

Step 3: Put an after post opt-in to appear at the end of every article.

Step 4: Add content upgrades on as many articles as you can.

(If you want to know more about opt-in forms, I have included a list of opt-in plugins for Wordpress along with helpful resources in the bonus material)

Undefeated Marketing Secret #20: To build an email list – put more opt-in forms.

---

21. No Incentive for Subscribers

Every website wants you to sign up for their newsletter. But, the problem is, most of us get more email newsletters than we ever read. We reach a point where we won't ever give our email address unless it's an offer we need really bad, something we've always wanted, a strong desire or solution to our worst problems.

That's why you see a lot of blogs giving away free eBooks, email courses, checklists and other useful resources that are valuable – unlike a newsletter whose content is unknown.

If you're like most people, you only sign up to email newsletters because the blog had a great incentive you wanted to download… then you stayed on the list because the stuff was good or because you're just too lazy to hit the unsubscribe button at the bottom of each email.

After all I've just said, it comes as no surprise that incentives increase your email opt-in rates substantially.

The best part?

It doesn't take much time to create one – it takes me about 2-6 hours for a short eBook.

A lot of people think it's supposed to be a perfect 50-page guide, when it could just be a 1 or 2 page checklist.

What you could do is, search for popular articles or info graphics and summarize them into quick checklists – remember that those articles are popular for a reason (hint: they are irresistible).

You can head over to Pinterest, go to a topic relevant to your industry and check out the top info graphics. To find the popular articles, you can get a free 2-week trial of buzzsumo.com and plug in all the blog domains relevant to your industry – if you don't know what blogs are popular in your industry, then search for them at alltop.com. Anyway, after you've typed the domain in the buzzsumo.com search box, you will get a list of the most popular blog posts for that blog, export the data so you can use it later… repeat for all the other blogs until you've gathered all data on the most popular content in your industry - now you can make something out of it.

Action Plan

Try your best to create an incentive (such as an eBook, checklist or email course) for your feature and sidebar opt-ins – these will be your two main offerings. You can add more as time goes by. Ensure you put a 3D picture of your incentive on the opt-in form so it looks tangible.

> **Undefeated Marketing Secret #21: Give people an incentive to attract them into your email list.**

22. Subscribing People Away

What does the word subscribe mean to you? According to Merriam Webster Dictionary, "to pay money to get a publication or service regularly".

It's something that costs money. Yet, many bloggers use it on their blogs for FREE updates and newsletters. But, why?

Well, I don't know. People just like to follow what they see on other popular blogs – blind following, that's what it is! Your subscriptions should see a slight increase once you exclude the word "subscribe".[7]

What are some better words?

• Get FREE Access
• Step Inside
• Get Exclusive Access
• Download

- Download Now

Anything that sounds less intimidating should work.

Action Plan

Exclude the word "subscribe" from all your opt-in form buttons and replace it with something less intimidating.

> *Undefeated Marketing Secret #22: Don't subscribe people away from your list.*

23. Not Testing

Everything must be tested. Always be testing, always be testing. Never make another move before testing. Be analytical. Marketers are analytical, they depend on data – and you're turning into a marketer yourself, so get used to it if you're haven't already.

Don't assume it's working. Test it against new things and never be satisfied with your results. Always refine your strategy and get better. You need to be innovative with your marketing. A lot of times, a few little changes in your copy or design can create tremendous differences.

Almost all opt-in plugins have built-in A/B testing, so you can test two or more different things at the same time. After some time, you'll find out that one of them is performing better than the other, when that happens, delete the bad performer and test the winner against another test – then repeat this process and never stop. Every day, you'll get better and better.

But, don't get too excited. Test one thing at a time. If you change 5 things at a time, you won't know what affected your results. It could have been any of the 5.

The last piece of advice is, give it some time. The longer the test lasts, the more accurate the results. For an email opt-in form, give it a week or two before you decide on the winner. Tweak both copy and design.

Action Plan

Test, tweak, test, repeat.

Undefeated Marketing Secret #23: ABT – Always Be Testing.

---

24. Ignoring Content Upgrades

Remember those little things you find in articles?
You know what that means for you right?
More work. But it's totally worth it.

For every article you'll write, you'll now need to create some bonuses to go with it – and like I said, it doesn't take much time to create a complimentary piece of document for each article. If you know what you're talking about in your article, then you'll easily come up with an upgrade idea. Take this as an example:

⭐ **Exclusive Bonus:** Download 37 Emotions That Sold the World on It

In the main blog post, I mentioned only 5 emotions that move people to buy. If people wanted to know all 37 emotions, then they would have to download it and join my email list. My subscriptions skyrocketed! That's why ignoring such a thing is the worst thing you'll ever do for your business.

Think about it!

It took me a few minutes to add those 37 words in a word document and send them to a freelancer (for $5) to make them look good. A lot of blogs don't even give anything exclusive as an upgrade, they just copy and paste the same article and offer it for download in case anyone wants to read it in pdf format. That is clever as well, especially for a step-by-step guide that someone would save for later use.

If you don't do content upgrades, you'll lose subscribers and if you lose subscribers, you'll make less money. If you make less money, you'll have to work harder – so at the end, content upgrades are actually for lazy smart people.

Action Plan

Purchase a content upgrade plugin and always add complimentary bonuses inside your articles – you can thank me later.

> *Undefeated Marketing Secret #24: Never be lazy with the content upgrade – otherwise, you'll pay for it later.*

3
DIRECT-RESPONSE & CONTENT MARKETING

This is my favorite part of the book because it's about writing. All you do here is write. Thousands of people have created 7 – 9 figure incomes just from writing – and you're next (If you do the work).

25. Not Guest Blogging

The first time I pitched a popular blog, my heart was beating pretty fast – not too fast, but fast enough for someone hiding behind a screen. Putting my words out there for the public to read and openly criticize was a fear I had. But, I thought to myself, what's the worst that could happen? Besides, I had no other choice if I wanted to succeed fast. So, I just went for it.

After the first time, the fear disappeared. Just like my first day of driving, I was a bit nervous, but the fear disappeared slowly every day I practiced – until it totally left (unless I'm driving like a maniac... but let's not get into that).

By the way, I didn't tell you the interesting part;

I got an E in grade 12 English. That's right, I almost failed English class upon graduating – yet, I was able to land popular blogs with ease.

But, I'm not saying this to brag. I'm trying to tell you that if someone that almost failed English class lands guest blogging opportunities on popular blogs – then so can you!

There's nothing better than showing your expertise and helping people online – and for free. You won't just build credibility and help people with your writing, but you'll also build your email list faster. In fact, Neil Patel built an 8-figure income through blogging. He says that he publishes 100 blog posts a year![8] But you don't have to go to that extreme... 1 – 4 a month should be an okay start.

You can't depend only on social media to expand your reach; you need to go to where your customers are. That means you need to be writing for the right blogs, the blogs that your customers read all the time. As master copywriter, Gary Halbert said, "If you and I owned a burger stand and were both in a contest to see who would sell more, what advantages would you have to help you win?"

Some people would say better meat, others would say sesame buns, and some will mention something about location and lower prices.

You know what Gary Halbert wanted? A Starving Crowd! That's exactly who you need to look for. The easiest way to find a hungry crowd is to go to a popular blog and read their popular blog posts, then read all the comments to view their reaction to the topic.

Remember that those 10 popular posts are popular because people found them helpful. But, sometimes in the comments, you'll see people asking other questions the writer forgot to answer... which is what you'll have to answer in the form of a blog post.

You should know the answer to their questions, if you don't, then conduct your research and learn until you become an expert in your field. If you want to stand out in your industry, you need to become the go-to expert. When someone asks for a [insert your industry] expert, then the first person that should come to their mind is you.

This is beginning to sound harder than you thought isn't it?

I want you to do so many things and you're not even half way through the book!

I know that feeling... but you wanted to become an UNDEFEATED marketer remember? Don't back out now. Like I said, if I can do it – you definitely can and you will! In fact, if you fail, it means I failed – and I won't let that happen.

So listen up, in the beginning, you found out whether your product is in demand… if it wasn't (in demand), you changed it. If it was (in demand), you positioned it well and made it unique. Then you identified your ideal buyer and learnt the ways to establish credibility and a track record for your product even if it's new to the market. You learnt that a website is a marketing tool and that it should be built by a marketing expert or under marketing supervision – so you already know more than most startup entrepreneurs. You also created a value ladder offering several products to old loyal customers – so your customer's long term value are a lot higher to you than many of your competitors (because you can sell them more stuff) – you also know that the deeper your value ladder, the better. Then you learnt about the popular types of opt-in forms so you can start to build your email list ASAP – in fact, you know about the feature box and the content upgrades that many startups take for granted (especially content upgrades). You actually know A LOT more than that, but I just wanted to be brief.

My point is, you've gotten this far! You've learnt more than what I knew when I first started my first ecommerce business and more than most first time and even intermediate entrepreneurs know about marketing.

To be honest with you, the knowledge isn't the hard part – it's the working part that really gets people. People just read these days and when it comes to applying what they learnt, they either procrastinate or give up because it's too much work!

What the…

Why did you start in the first place?

They'll usually say something like "well, I never thought it would be THIS hard!"

True, but bad excuse. Because starting a company is known to be harder than any full time job, if it wasn't, then everyone would most likely be an entrepreneur. The only difference is that entrepreneurs have a dream that they work to turn into a reality while others just talk.

Now that you're back in business, it's time to get writing and help people with your writing!

Action Plan

Step 1: Choose 3 from the following 11 popular blog categories (pick the closest if there is no perfect match or only one if it is the perfect match).
• Business & Entrepreneurship
• Marketing
• Social Media & Blogging
• Personal Finance
• Freelancing
• Career
• Self-Improvement
• Gadgets & Technology
• Creative Endeavors
• Parenting
• News, Culture & Entertainment

Step 2: Create a list of all the popular blogs from the categories you chose previously. You can search for blogs by either typing "[category] blog" in Google or searching for them in AllTop.com (I have included a list of 5 popular blogs from each category that pass all requirements from steps 2- 4)

Step 3: Now, it's time to filter the good from the bad – the ones worth writing for and the ones you should never write for.

FIRST, do they let you add a link back to your landing page? This one is easy to find out, just open a blog post and look if there are any links back to the writer's website or social media accounts – it should look like this:

Written by Tim Ferriss   Topics Entrepreneurship, Marketing

This story is about the launch of Harry's, a new men's grooming brand.

Specifically, it will explain how they gathered nearly 100,000 email addresses in one

Look at how Tim's blog links to Harry's website. In fact, he's done it several times throughout the post. This would be a good target... except that... fourhourworkweek.com is an advanced blog. Anyway, that's one way popular blogs can link to your website. The other way is like this:

Zak Mustapha

Z   Zak Mustapha is on a lifelong mission to help entrepreneurs learn from other entrepreneurs mistakes. Download his FREE 101 Legendary Books to become a Hero Entrepreneur (Even if You're a Total Beginner) to know the exact books an entrepreneur like you must read.

They give you a small box at the end or at the beginning of your article and allow you to put a link in it. Just make sure it's visible and not way deep down the page or on another page... no one is going to go the extra mile to search for your bio if it's not directly under or on top of the blog post.
SECOND, do they have an engaged audience? Since there is no point having a link if the audience isn't active or the blog doesn't get much traffic in the first place (because no

one would click on it). To find out the level of engagement, we look at two things. 1) The number of comments (anything above 5 comments per post on average is good). 2) The number of shares (anything above 50 shares per post is good).

THIRD, do they accept guest posts in the first place? There are 2 ways to find out. 1) Look on their website for any buttons in the menu or footer where it says, "Write for us", "Contribute" or anything to that meaning. 2) Search on Google for any clues since some blogs do accept guest posts but they don't say it. If you find that their posts are written by different authors, go ahead and search, "urlin: [blogname.com] guest blogging" or "urlin: [blogname.com] write for us"... just change the last word to "contribute", "guest post" and "guidelines" etc. You should then get results for their guidelines page that looks something like this:

We just found the page for the requirements. This means they accept guest posts. If they don't, move on to the next blog.

Step 4: Update your list by adding all the blogs that credit you well, have an engaged audience and accept guest posts. Remove the blogs that don't.

Step 5: Look for the 10 most popular blog posts on just 3 of those blogs (take 3 at a time to stay focused). You can find them on the side bar like this:

POPULAR ARTICLES:

The #1 Conversion Killer in Your Copy (and How to Beat It)

10 Ways to Build Authority as an Online Writer

What Is Content Marketing?

The 7 Essential Elements of Effective Social Media Marketing

How to Immediately Become a More Productive (and Better) Writer

The Perfect Anatomy of a Modern Web Writer [Infographic]

Or sign up for the buzzsumo.com trial version and type the blog's name in the search. You will get a list of the popular blogs that looks like this:

Export the results to Excel and repeat this for all the blogs on your list even though you only need 3 for now, but don't forget; you're on a 2 week trial version, so collect all the data now. Personally, I would recommend at least, 10 blogs.

Step 6: Read the top 10 articles from the 3 blogs you chose to focus on, so you can get to know more about the audience's fears and desires. (You're reading these to get ideas for what to write, so make sure you write down a list of questions found in the comments section and all the fears and desires the article itself solves). Great writers read and write a lot.

Step 7: After you've got yourself some ideas on what to write, send your pitch or post to the blog (depending on what the guidelines say. Read them before pitching, since some blogs require you to send a full post and not a pitch).

Step 8: It should take around a week or two (sometimes less) to get a reply so ensure you contact 3 blogs at the same time, you don't want to just depend on one. Send a kind follow up email after 2 weeks if you get no response... move to the next blog.

Step 9: Write your post after you receive a green light from the blog's editor.

Step 10: Put one link to your landing page in the bio. The more links you put, the less clicks you get, the slower it will take to build your email list. Also keep your bio short; First sentence about yourself and the benefit you give readers (by mentioning what you do for them) and second sentence will tell people to download our incentive. Like this:

> **About the Author:** Mary Fernandez is a self-proclaimed "blogoholic" on a mission to help other bloggers stop twiddling their thumbs and start getting measurable results. For more standout strategies (and other blogging tricks besides), check out her new Persuasive Bloggers Mastermind group.

Let's break that up...

Credibility: Mary is a self-proclaimed "blogaholic"

Benefit: On a mission to help other bloggers stop twiddling their thumbs and start getting measurable results.

Incentive: For more standout strategies (and other blogging tricks besides), check out her new Persuasive Bloggers Mastermind group.

Step 11: Once your article is published, check to see how many people signed up to your email list. If you get nothing after one or two guest posts, then ignore that blog and move on to the next. Don't waste your time on a blog that gets you nothing in return.

> *Undefeated Marketing Secret #25: Guest blogging is the best way to growth hack your blog free.*

26. Rushing Through The Headline

Come on, it's just a headline, how hard can it be?

What's the first thing that grabs your attention to a blog post, book or sales letter? It's the title right? For that reason, the headline is critical. Because if your headline just misses the spot a tiny bit, your whole writing goes to waste – because no one will read it, or even worse – the wrong people will.

Your headline should sell the idea in just a few words – usually eight words (although it can be more or less). The headline must hook the reader instantly. Such a headline isn't written in just a few minutes, it can take hours. In fact, if you were to spend 80% of your time on the headline and 20% on the main article, your time would not be wasted.

The best I've heard on headlines is from master copywriter David Ogilvy who said, "If you haven't done some selling in your headline, you have wasted 80 percent of your client's money." Ogilvy knew that headlines are what grab people to read.

You might as well not bother with writing if you're not going to make any effort to perfect your headline.

How do you write a killer headline?

There are different types of headlines and the topic of headlines is wide. For the sake of simplicity, I'm going to show you only two types of headlines because it can really get overwhelming especially for an entrepreneur who has to run a business. So let's dig right in.

The most popular headlines are the "How to" and list headlines. [9]

How to Headlines

How to [Blank]

How to Be [Desirable Quality]

How to [Blank] (Even if [Common Obstacle])

How to [Blank] Without [Objectionable Action]

How to [Do Something] While You [Do Something Else]

How to [Blank] and [Blank]

How to Use [Blank] to [Blank]

List headlines

[X] Ways to [Do Something]

[X] Surprising Reasons [Blank]

[X] Steps to [Goal or Achievement]

[X] Tips for [Doing Something]

[X] Resources for [Audience/Process]

[X] [Blanks] for [Blank]

[X] [Blank] Secrets Every [Target Audience] Should Know

After you've filled in the blanks, your headline will look like most headlines you see on blogs, so you need to tweak it to make it stand out. For that to happen, your headline needs to be:

Strong and Specific

For example, let me use the third list headline; [X] Steps to [Goal or Achievement].

7 Steps to Building a 7-Figure Business

That looks good and it's interesting to the reader (because you're reading a book on marketing, you obviously find this headline interesting. You would be the typical audience for such a topic). But it still looks like a headline everyone has seen, so let's see if we can add any of those 2 ingredients to it.

Strong and Specific

Update #1: 7 Steps to Building a 7-Figure Business in 13 Months

Isn't that a bit better? It's more specific and sounds like the writer knows what he's talking about. But, we can make it better.

Update #2: 7 Proven Steps to Building a 7-Figure Business in 13 Months

That's much better than the previous one because we've powered it with the word "proven". This one is stronger and sparks more emotion, but can we do better? Of course, however, that's enough to land major blogs such as the Huffington Post.

But, wait! I didn't give you a list with words that can strengthen your headline. There are too many to count. So the list I'm going to give you isn't all there is. Anyway, here are 20:[10]

1. Discover
2. Easy
3. Free
4. New
5. Proven
6. Save
7. Results
8. It's Here
9. Introducing
10. At Last
11. Guarantee
12. Bargain
13. Last Chance
14. Quick
15. Sale
16. Why
17. How to
18. Just Arrived
19. Now

20.   Announcing

Action Plan

Craft your headline with mastery even if it takes hours –
most people are lazy. Ensure you make it specific and
powerful. Practice daily.

> **Undefeated Marketing Secret #26: Practice writing
> headlines daily and you will achieve mastery soon enough.**

27.   Your Content Isn't Easy to Scan

Do you always read an article from top to bottom or do
you scan to see if it's interesting first?
Most readers scan, even when reading a book, they check
out the contents page first. People won't bother reading it
if the subheads are uninteresting or confusing.
Another thing to note is; readers won't always be
interested in every single point you make. They'll scan it
and then read the points they're interested in. That's why
if you treat every subhead like a mini-headline, you'll
write stronger copy. So, your job for writing headlines
doesn't end with the main headline, but also the subheads.

Action Plan

Use subheads to highlight your ideas and make your copy
manageable.

> *Undefeated Marketing Secret #27: Subheads are the most important part of writing after the main headline.*

28. Your Ideas are Weak

If you read the Google results for "[xx] tips for [blank]", you'll realize a lot of the ideas within most articles are the same old weak crap ones that everyone else says. Same tips, same everything. You won't stand out if you're saying the exact same as everyone else. Weak ideas are not appealing.

Even if you implement every trick in the book, it won't matter at all if your ideas are old, weak and boring. If you want people to pay attention to what you say (online and offline), then you should have mind-blowing ideas. Grammar and vocabulary isn't what makes people read your writing. They read it because it has ideas that will help them. No matter how excellent your sentence is, if it doesn't illuminate the reader, delete it.

Of course, you won't reinvent the wheel, but you'll still be able to give your perspective of things and personal experiences of what works and what doesn't.

Action Plan

Make sure each of the ideas you list as subheads are intriguing ideas and not the same old boring stuff found everywhere.

> *Undefeated Marketing Secret #28: People read for ideas.*

29. Opening with a Boring Tone

Everyone makes mistakes; it's not something to feel bad about. – Boring!

There's a lot of ways to write an opening. – Also boring.

They have no clue, do they?

These famous bloggers, they jump right into the topic.

They forget to tell you about the hard times you've been through, the frustration you're going through right now with your business how you're starting to feel a bit hopeless... like you'll never succeed in your life.

That regardless of how hard you've tried, it just doesn't seem to work out.

But, that's not the worst part. The worst part is, you don't know what's going on! It's burning you! You demand some answers NOW!

Why does my competition win even though they don't do anything special? How can I get customers to buy from me? Why don't people come to my store?

Wait; let's back it up a bit...

So how do you write an opening that will grab the reader's attention?

You read back their thoughts.

You see those frustrations and desires people have? Those are what you talk about in the beginning.

For example, your reader is someone who struggles to lose fat and she's tried every single diet you can think of. Here's how you could open it:

"Admit it... you've done it all.

You ate everything they told you to eat and done every exercise they told you to do. Yet, no matter what you do, those love handles don't want to go away.

At some point, you start to wonder...

Do you need to be patient to see results?

Or is there something these experts haven't told you?"

Okay, so that's the end of the opening.

See what I did there? I sounded like a shrink, repeating the readers' thoughts and what they're going through. In other words, I understood them and empathized with them. In fact, this opening is called the empathetic opening.

Let me tell you something I should have told you before; your headline isn't enough! Your headline is only what gets them to click on your article or open up your letter – but your opening is what pulls them in.

In other words, headlines get clicks and openings get read. - Take a note of that.

Then there's another thing I have to tell you that you're probably forgetting; you're not the only one out there that's written on the topic. Your readers have already read every single piece of content on the subject but nothing seems to work for them – they want someone who gets it. That means even after they click to read what you have to say, they'll be hovering over the back button looking for a reason to exit – because they've heard everything.

So how do you get readers hooked onto your post?

You empathize with them. (Like you would do with a friend)

These days, everyone wants to shove their ideas down your throat – they lack empathy.

But, isn't everyone different?

Everyone thinks their situation is unique. But, the truth is most people are pretty much the same... just like the fat loss problem, it resonates with a lot of people. They exercise and diet hard, but struggle to get a flat stomach.

Sure, the fat loss programs work for the first few weeks or months, but those final pounds feel impossible to drop.

We are all human and we go through the same problems, but everyone wants to believe they're special.

So, the secret to writing empathetic openings is…

Know what they're going through and write it down to them!

Action Plan

Go through the top 10 blogs, read them all along with the comments and listen to what people are saying. Then write back their thoughts in the opening. (I've already mentioned this, haven't I?)

> **Undefeated Marketing Secret #29: Be empathetic with your opening and the rest of your copy.**

30. Ending it With a Lame Tone or a Question

So you've learnt about headlines, subtitles, openings and the importance of strong ideas. Now it's time for the ending. Remember that at the end, you want people to take action to whatever you're offering at the bottom – not just read and close the article.

Have you seen those people who end their blog posts with a question?

Do you think anyone is even bothered to answer their questions? Out of hundreds of likes or shares, you'll probably find just a few comments and usually those comments are not answers to the question. Because a lot of write-ups on the internet end with questions, people have become blind to it – they just don't care about it anymore – they think it's just how writers end their articles and not something they should really answer.

People are usually half-asleep while surfing the web. So asking them to write their answers is a huge task.

I contribute to several popular blogs and some of their editors weaken the ending with some lame question that gets hardly any replies – yet the shares are in the hundreds! I just don't get it! Who said a blog post should end with a question? What's the wisdom behind it?

Obviously, there is no wisdom behind it. It is only blind-following and a viral disease that has spread.

So how do you end a blog post?

Well, you wake your reader!

How do you awaken them? You end with a powerful motivating tone. In other words, you become a motivational coach at the end of the post.

Your ending should give them a burst of energy and inspire them to do what you just taught them to do. And since writers who write this way are kind of rare – readers will feel different towards YOU, because you're the only writer that understands them and the only writer that energized them. Those readers will be intrigued to know who wrote the article and therefore, click on your landing page to download your free offer (and get on your email list).

Action Plan

End your articles with a boom! This is where you smack your reader to wake.

> **Undefeated Marketing Secret #30: Motivational Endings will energize people to take action.**

31. Not Proofreading

Have you ever read bad Amazon reviews for books? If you have, you've probably seen a lot of complaints about grammar and spelling mistakes (maybe for this book too). They hate on the whole article or book just because of a few typos and minor errors. These kinds of people are foolish.

Either way, that doesn't give you a reason to be careless. Always make sure spelling is correct and that your words make sense.

Action Plan

Read and edit your content or let a professional editor do it. Hiring an editor doesn't make you a fake, many of the stuff you read online goes through an editor, including this book! (So if you see any grammar mistakes, blame it on my editor!)

> **Undefeated Marketing Secret #31: Edit or the Grammar police will bust you.**

32. Lying & Exaggerating

If you guarantee your product is unbreakable, it better live up to its promise. Some people will try hard to prove you wrong. If they do, you're going to lose your trustworthiness and may even get sued. Sometimes, it also makes you look stupid. Look at this:

Dr. Cafe's Tagline "The best coffee in the world"...
So what do you think? Doesn't that sound like the cheesiest claim ever? The person who thought of that tagline must have been the most uninformed marketing/branding person ever.

Action Plan

Head over to your website, social media accounts and all other platforms and tone down on the exaggerations. Delete anything that goes overboard and could deteriorate your credibility.

Undefeated Marketing Secret #32: Be honest. Be real.

---

33. Selling Features

No one cares about features! Remember these three points:
• People like to buy but hate being sold to.
• People buy for emotional reasons not rational.
• Once they are sold, they assure themselves with logic.
And...
Features are Rational
Benefits are Emotional
Let's see an example of a product being promoted for its features:
"Dr. Frank's shampoo comes in a 250ml brown bottle and contains natural ingredients such as honey, olive oil, Argan oil, aloe leaves and much more. Get yours now for just $8.99."
Does that sound like something you'd buy? Maybe if you're a hardcore fan of natural ingredients. But, most people don't care about natural ingredients – not because they hate natural ingredients, but because they don't know the benefits. So let's try highlighting the benefits for the same product:

"Dr. Frank's shampoo is made from natural ingredients, which gently infuse into your hair and scalp giving you that gorgeous look. Because it's such a rare product, you'll truly stand out from the crowd as the one with beautiful hair. The 250ml brown bottle it comes in; means that it will last for long duration of time before you'll need another one."

Isn't that better? It strikes people's emotions. People buy shampoo to look good and buy a 250ml bottle because it lasts longer than the 100ml bottle. As you can see, we blended features along with benefits so people can rationalize after they've (emotionally) bought and convince themselves that they bought it because of the natural ingredients.

PS: We could have done better, but I just wanted to keep it basic.

Action Plan

Use benefits, then help people satisfy their logic by blending in the features.

Undefeated Marketing Secret #33: Sell them with emotions by using benefits – then give them features to satisfy their logic.

---

34. Being Subtle

Do you know the difference between non-direct response marketing and direct response marketing?

Well, non-direct response is like a TV commercial, they don't have a call to action; they are subtle. It's usually something cool, funny and short. I'm sure there are some advertisements that you still remember till this day. But, the problem with these advertisements is that they don't tell you to buy anything and even if they did, results are impossible to measure.

A non-direct response advertisement can't be measured – so you can't find out the return on your investment.

On the other hand, direct response marketing promotions have calls to action and can be measured to the dollar. You can know exactly how many people responded to the advertisement. Direct response makes people take their credit card out and buy immediately. Not tomorrow or next week. But immediately!

So now that you know the difference:

Non-direct response advertisements are subtle. While direct response advertisements are not – they are direct.

Being subtle confuses people… being direct shows them the clear path they should take.

Being able to measure an advertisement is extremely important, because without measuring, how would you know if something was working or not?

You've probably seen a lot of TV commercials that didn't make any sense. It was just a waste of your time and a waste of the advertisers' money.

And the worst part?

They don't even know if the commercial made them any sales or not!

Action Plan

Don't be subtle. Be direct and always add a call to action.

> *Undefeated Marketing Secret #34: Calls to action make people buy on the spot or never rather than maybe or never.*

35. Assuming the Customer Knows Their Problem

Most customers don't know their problem. If they did, they would have found a solution for it... but they haven't... yet.

This is where you come in. Similar to the opening we used for writing a blog post, you replay what they are going through with your words. Address and acknowledge the pain they are experiencing.

A lot of businesses jump right into the solution and forget to explain what problem the solution solves. People will just ignore the solution because they don't see how relevant it is to them.

Action Plan

Address the problem, and then present your product as the solution to their problem.

> *Undefeated Marketing Secret #35: Problem comes before solution.*

36. Assuming The Customer Trusts You

Thanks to advertisers, consumers have become more skeptical than ever. They won't trust a word you say, no matter how awesome your product will make them feel, they'll always think there is something you're not telling them. And with skepticism like that, ordinary proof is not enough.

So how can you convince a skeptical prospect?

The first thing you do is assume they are skeptical and address every single objection they could possibly have.

The next thing you should do is, always offer superior proof. Proof that no one else has ever offered before.

When you say good stuff about yourself or product, you're only stating an opinion. But, when a satisfied customer says something good about you, then it becomes a fact. Social proof is the strongest proof you can offer a prospect.

Let's say I'm selling a fitness product and I put a picture of a guy with six-pack abs – you'll think, yeah, that's cool. But, if I were to show you a picture of that same guy except this time, it's a 6 month old photo of him when he was fat... your reaction will be totally different... you'd be amazed.

The before and after pictures offer stronger proof than the picture with six-pack abs. alone.

Another thing people believe is technology and science.

If your product has technology, then give your new technology a name and explain its unique benefits to the audience.

If your product has some science behind it, you should back up your claims with scientific research and mention the authority of the doctors who conducted the research. You'll piggyback their credibility this way.

Here's a fictional product called Zimbotech, a treadmill with AI technology:

Zimbotech is the treadmill of the future! With its Ultra-AI technology, it will analyze your body and give you the ideal running experience... something even Olympic athletes don't have yet.... Blah blah blah....

According to Dr. Famous Guy's latest research, "97.3% of people don't know how to run on a treadmill, they run at the wrong speeds and bad timings, and most of those people include fitness experts."

Proof like that is superior to a random testimonial.

Action Plan:

Step 1: Get the list of competitors you gathered in the beginning of this book and go through their sales pages, take a note of all the proofs they use to back up their claims. Make note of every single one, the more, the better.

Step 2: After you've got a list of "proofs", look at how you can make your proof stronger. Superior proof will crush all the mediocre proof available in the market.

> *Undefeated Marketing Secret #36: Go the extra mile in backing up your claims – stronger proof makes you stronger.*

37. Using Weak Words

Not all words are equal in power. For example, the word "burn" is a powerful word. It sparks a powerful emotion. Add power words in your headlines, articles, subheads and whatever you get your hands on. There's no explanation for this, but here's a list of some words:

- Panic
- Deadly
- Conquer
- Crush
- Caution
- Stunning
- Secure
- Horrific
- Sinful
- Hidden
- Disgusting
- Free
- Billion
- Insider
- Amazing

Action Plan

Incorporate power words to make your copy stronger than ever.

> **Undefeated Marketing Secret #37: Power your words with power words.**

38. Skipping Steps

You don't yell "bombs away" and throw your offer on the first line of your copy. It's done later on... once you hit their emotions and build up their desire for your product, then you can slam your offer.

You can't skip steps in selling...

In fact, there are four main pieces in a sales letter: Promise, Picture, Proof and Push.

Promise: Promise them a valuable and powerful benefit. This is usually done in the headline and first few paragraphs of the copy. For example, "How I Made $4,200 in 5 days Without any Special Skill". Making money without the need for any special skill is the promise here.

Picture: Painting a picture in the prospects mind of how his life will be different when he achieves the promised benefit. For example, "...after you learn my money making system for ordinary people, you'll never need to worry about finding a job anymore. You'll have plenty of time and money left for your family. Even the struggling business people will envy you, they'll want to know your little secret. In fact, people will pay YOU for what you know...." The prospect will start to see himself with product in his possession, how his life has positively changed and he'll find it hard to live without it. His desire will increase for the product, the more we tell him about these life changing benefits.

Proof: This is where all the science, technology, testimonials, case studies and all the proof "stuff" I've told you about previously comes in. (#10 and #36)

Push: Also known as, the offer... is where you slam your offer and remove all the risk with a strong guarantee.

You can simplify the steps if you need to (or you're just lazy) but you can never EVER skip any of the four pieces of the sales letter. In building terms, your foundation is the promise, the brick is your picture, the concrete is your proof and your roof is your offer or push.

Action Plan

Stick with the structure and don't skip any steps in the sales process.

> *Undefeated Marketing Secret #38: You can only simplify steps. Never skip.*

39. You Don't Have a Story

In Tested Advertising Methods, master copywriter, John Caples says that he recommends 13 out of the 19 types of copy – story copy was one of them. He said, "This copy starts off with a human-interest situation. Then comes a story, the moral of which is 'Buy the product advertised'". Before you start your story, you need to know your audience better than they know themselves. Otherwise, how would you know what kind of story would make them move? If you can't find out what makes your prospect connect with your story, then your copy won't work.

But, how do you find your story?

- Speak with the manufacturer's product engineer and find out the production process from start to finish, as well as special specs that make the product unique.

- Your own story of how you started and where your product came from etc.

- Latest news. Nothing like talking about the current events and putting your product in the picture.

- Use testimonials that you received from your first sales – your customer could be your story. (The Federal Trade Commission regulates Testimonials; visit their website ftc.gov for legal information. This book is not a legal advisor).

After you've figured out what your story will be about, I need to tell you something;

Do you want to know how to become great at writing copy?

Read copy, hand write copy, practice copy. I could give you all the tricks and theories there is, but there's nothing like actually reading previous successful control letters and writing them by hand several times – read each letter at least, 10 times and hand copy it 5 times (yeah, you read that right). But, don't just read and write for the sake of it. Pay attention to how the paragraphs and sentences are structured, the intentional grammar mistakes, types of words used, what the PS says, what parts are emphasized, etc.

The reason you write and read it so many times is because you want to engrave it into your brain. Of course, you want to engrave great copy into your mind – not the crap ones. In the bonus material, I have included 10 best sales letters of all time so you can start honing your skills.

After you've honed your skills, here's the structure of how your story copy should look like:

Opening: Start with the most exciting part of the story.

Body: Bring up the problem and slowly walk him to the solution.

Close: Finally! You have found a solution.

Remember to move fast throughout your story so you don't bore your reader with a slow story.

Action Plan

Step 1: Find your story.

Step 2: Hand copy successful letters – until you engrave them in your brain.

Step 3: Move fast through your story – but don't sacrifice it for detail (detail is important). e.g. 1970 Dodge Charger R/T instead of saying a car.

Step 4: Remember the structure... don't skip it.

> *Undefeated Marketing Secret #39: The best sales letter ever written was a powerful story that people could relate to – Two Young Men.*

40. Having No Big Idea

What's the big idea behind your story? There has to be one. Let's take a look at Two Young Men by The Wall Street Journal, for example;

Dear Reader:

On a beautiful late spring afternoon, twenty-five years ago, two young men graduated from the same college. They were very much alike, these two young men. Both had been better than average students, both were personable and both – as young college graduates are, were filled with ambitious dreams for the future.

Recently, these two men returned to college for their 25th reunion.

They were still very much alike. Both were happily married. Both had three children. And both, it turned out, had gone to work for the same Midwestern manufacturing company after graduation, and were still there.

But there was a difference. One of the men was manager of a small department of that company. The other was its president.

What Made The Difference

Have you ever wondered, as I have, what makes this kind of difference in people's lives? It isn't always a native intelligence or talent or dedication. It isn't that one person wants success and the other doesn't.

The difference lies in what each person knows and how he or she makes use of that knowledge.

And that is why I am writing to you and to people like you about The Wall Street Journal. For that is the whole purpose of The Journal: To give its readers knowledge – knowledge that they can use in business.

...

This is just a portion of the best sales letter of all time that generated $2 billion in revenue for WSJ.

Anyway, what's the big idea behind this letter?

Well, it's that knowledge lets you advance ahead of people and achieve success in business.

Your sales letter should also have a big idea behind it. Once you go over the sales letters that I've included in the bonus material, you'll find out that each one of them has a big idea behind it.

Action Plan

Step 1: Read all 10 sales letters that I've included in the bonus material.

Step 2: Get your notebook out and write the big idea behind each one.

Step 3: Now that you've grasped the idea or big ideas. Sit down and think of your big idea, then write it down. It may take time, so don't worry if you can't think of anything now. Learn more about your prospect, product and just take a walk outside for inspiration. Don't forget, the idea must appeal to the prospect.

Undefeated Marketing Secret #40: Have a big idea in your copy.

---

41. Talking With a Corporate Voice

When you write a sales letter, a lot of people switch into a weird corporate voice. They start to sound like a letter from the bank. That's not how killer copy is written. No one trusts a bank. People trust other people they know. You must talk to prospects in a friendly conversational tone like you would do with a friend – so they can trust you like a friend.

You've been taught at school to write in formal – but that advice doesn't work in copywriting. In copywriting, you write like you talk.

Although, I have to admit, you won't write exactly the way you speak – but it will be very close. When writing, imagine your prospect is sitting in front of you and you're conversing with him about the product.

After reading the 10 sales letters from the bonus material, you'll realize they have a very conversational tone.

Action Plan

Step 1: Read the 10 sales letters aloud to know how powerful copy should sound like.

Step 2: When writing sales copy, imagine the prospect is right in front of you and you're talking to him, enthusiastically telling him about the product.

> **Undefeated Marketing Secret #41: Write as you talk.**

42. Not Using Numbers Wisely

Instead of saying, "The average human spends 10 minutes brushing their teeth every day. Our 30-second toothbrush saves you 7 minutes a day".

Say, "The average person spends 3.5 years of his life brushing their teeth. What could you do in 3.5 years? Our 30-second toothbrush gives you cleaner teeth and 2 years of your life back".

Note that my numbers were only guesses.

If you ever do invent the 30-second toothbrush, then I'd be happy to know. Drop me a tweet @zakmustapha.

Action Plan

Use numbers that people can understand and feel. E.g. Instead of saying 21,000 die from hunger every day, say 14 die every minute – it's easier to grasp and more powerful.

> **Undefeated Marketing Secret #42: Present numbers in interesting ways.**

43. Think You Deserve Attention

You don't deserve attention. You have to earn it all the time. When you write a new blog post, launch a new product or make a new announcement, no one other than your hardcore fans will give you their attention. Just because you've done something good to them in the past, doesn't mean they'll pay attention to everything you say in the future. People are busy and they won't turn around to see what you've got to say unless it's worth their attention.

Follow the AIDA formula...

Attention
Interest
Desire
Action

Attention is the first stage of the buyer's journey. If you fail to grab their attention, you've failed at everything. In fact, the reason why headlines are so important is that they grab attention.

What do you use to grab someone's attention?

Pictures, graphics, videos, words and sound.

But, everyone uses the same thing, so people have become blind to it. Businesses are always trying to get people's attention with their advertisements – they are everywhere – just look out the window and count how many advertisements there are. Some work, some don't.

You obviously won't be able to grab everyone's attention, that's why you should only focus on grabbing your target buyer's attention – no one else.

So how do you grab someone's attention?

Be different.

That's it! You could put an oversized attention grabbing image, a 3D info graphic that pops out the screen and/or powerful words such as FREE that grab people's attention... anything surprising.

There's plenty of ways to do it; just look at what your competitors are doing and do the complete opposite and you'll get their attention.

I have to tell you something before you go and try this. KNOW YOUR CUSTOMER. If you don't know them well, you may offend them with your difference. The better you know someone, the better you'll be at moving them through the AIDA framework.

Action Plan

Use different words, pictures, graphics, videos and sound to get people's attention. Then navigate them through the AIDA framework using an interesting offer to keep them reading, create a desire to make them want the product, then lead them to take action and buy (or click or whatever you want them to do).

> *Undefeated Marketing Secret #43: Be different to earn their attention every time.*

44. Little Belief in What you Sell

Remember when I told you about passion in the beginning?

This is what I also meant...

If you don't believe in what you sell, you won't confidently recommend people to buy it – there will be this slight hesitant tone in your voice or a lack of enthusiasm.

The most important thing in selling is...................

Believing that buying your product is the best thing a customer can do for himself.

That's one of the most important part of selling. You should make your customer feel like a hero in your story copy (and other types of copy). Because he made such a great decision buying your product, he is now a hero... he overcame his problem (the villain). Tell him how his family will be so proud of his action, how his future self will thank him, etc.

And if he doesn't, then his villain (the problem) will overcome him.

So, you wanna sell?

Make it the decision of their life.

Action Plan

Believe in what you sell, and show the customer that buying your product is one of the best things they'll do in their life. Don't sell what you wouldn't recommend. You're not a dope dealer – the "don't get high on your own supply" mentality doesn't work in the legal market.

Undefeated Marketing Secret #44: Buying your product should be the best thing people will do in their lives.

4
SEO & INBOUND MARKETING

Inbound marketing is the opposite of outbound marketing. Outbound focuses on you broadcasting your message and acquiring leads. But, inbound is where you put content on your site and customers come to you. This is what happens when you write a blog post on your blog. People search in Google for a solution to their problem, they find results (hopefully, yours), they read them and may subscribe to your email list if your content was mind blowing.

But, to get people finding your business's blog in the first place, you need to appear in the Google search results. In order to appear in the Google search results, your site and content must be search engine optimized. Search Engine Optimization (SEO) is a process for getting organic search engine traffic.

Almost all search results you find in Google use some sort of SEO to show up in search results. Google has a 63.9% market share, Bing has 20.7 and Yahoo has 12.7% as of

October 2015... for that reason, we will focus on Google only.

Ranking on the first few results on Google will send you loads of traffic, it also makes your customers trust you because you were a top result. The main tactic for SEO is plugging in keywords that the search engine will read. However, due to competition, it's a lot harder than just a few words. This chapter will address the mistakes made by many SEO beginners and show you how to rank on the first page.

45. Filling Content With Keywords

You see, search engines don't understand your content – you need to insert keywords relevant to the topic. For example, if someone searches for "Indian Restaurant in New York", I'll need to include those keywords somewhere on my website to appear in the search results. Of course, it's a lot more complicated than that. However, many people go overboard and fill up their content with as many keywords as they can – it used to work. But when Google released its Panda update in 2011, a lot of websites that stuffed their "thin" content with too many keywords got penalized. The update was made to stop poor content from ranking in the top.

Google updates its algorithm regularly. According to Moz, Google makes 500-600 changes each year. To get the recent updates go to https://moz.com/google-algorithm-change

People who stuff their content with keywords put themselves in danger.

BUT, WHY IS GOOGLE SO STRICT?

Simply because they want users to find quality answers to their problems. For that reason, if you create content for the user rather than create it for Google – you won't go wrong.

To be honest, most of the time, I don't think about putting in keywords in my articles until I've finished writing my post. In fact, almost all the time, I end up including the keywords unintentionally. If I write about "healthy British fish pie", I'm obviously going to include "healthy British fish pie" in my article… makes sense, right?

Anyway, if you use wordpress.org, then you've just made things easier for yourself. You can just download a plugin called Yoast SEO, enter a keyword you want to rank for and it quickly checks if you've included that in your content – it gives you a green light when you're good to go, red light when it's bad... and yellow light if it's "OK". See figure below...

Your Google rankings are influenced by several factors and having the right keywords is just one of them. In fact, if you just rely on keywords, you won't get any traffic. You need to make people share it, talk about it and also link to it.

In other words, you need traffic, links, shares, keywords... (Plus some others)

Action Plan

Include keyword in the title, body, Meta description, images alt text and URL (Use hyphens to separate URLs).

> *Undefeated Marketing Secret #45: Optimize with keywords in moderation.*

46. Putting Images, Videos and Flash Without Text

Search engines are not able to "understand" what your image, video or flash site is supposed to be. That's why you need to include, text under it.

Action Plan

For images, add alt text, for videos, put transcript under the video, and everything else with html text.

> *Undefeated Marketing Secret #46: Optimize non-text content with text.*

47. Relying on Keywords Only

Keywords are a main factor in determining how relevant your content is. However, depending only on it isn't enough to make you rank. Your ranking depends on two things;
- Relevance
- Popularity

Relevance is through selecting the right keywords. But, what about popularity? How do you make your post popular?

Simple… promote it!

Get links, get shares etc.

However, not all links are equal. A link from Huffington Post has higher value than a link from an unknown small site. That's why you need to focus on getting links from popular websites if you want your links to become popular too.

Some websites have earned a high level of trust with Google. These websites get preferential treatment. But, that shouldn't be bad news for you because you'll use them to get links and increase your own website's trust.

In fact, this is one of the benefits of guest blogging; you get to include your link in your bio on the popular blog that you write for. Not only does it send you traffic, but also affects your ranking and trustworthiness with Google.

> **Undefeated Marketing Secret #47: Let trustworthy websites testify for your trustworthiness to search engines.**

48. Writing Rubbish Content Just for The Sake of Consistency

So what is great quality content?

It's a very vague term, but it's a lot easier than explaining it – that's why I and a lot of people love to do it. Except this time, in this book, right now, for you, I'll explain not only what it is, but also how to get ideas so you can create quality content. Okay, here it is:

Great quality content is educational content that is relevant and helpful to its reader.

- Relevant – Is it what the potential customer is looking for? Does it address a desire or problem they have?
- Helpful – Does it over deliver what you promised? (Remember that just delivering isn't what makes content great – your content needs to over deliver the promise).

To be honest, helpfulness depends on you. Nobody can really "teach" it. Just go the extra mile in helping people.

But, relevance... that's another thing. In fact, that's the whole purpose of this section. To find relevant topics.

Action Plan

We're going to use the Keyword Planner from Google AdWords so we can find keywords that have a decent amount of search volume. I believe Google AdWords went through a recent update, although I couldn't find any announcements about the update online, I just woke and found the interface looked a bit different.

KEYWORD SEARCH
- Go to the Google Keyword Planner Tool (http://adwords.google.com/keywordplanner) and create an account if you don't have one already.
- You may have to enter billing information. You can pause the campaign and they won't charge you.
- Click on "Tools" and select "Keyword Planner" from the dropdown menu.
- Click on "Search for new keywords using a phrase, website or category".
- In the "Your product or service" box, write down your 2 to 3 keywords related to the topic you want

to write about. Don't be broad by typing, "money". Instead, try to narrow it down to "how to make money".

- In "Your Landing Page", I would just keep it empty unless you want it to find keywords from your existing content.
- In "Your Product Category" you can put the category your business/product is in and Google will bring up some suggested keywords based on your category in case you forgot some.
- Now select the country you want to target. Although it is a blog post, you want to avoid wasting time on people who won't buy from you (if you're based in France, then put France as your country). If you're online based and you serve customers worldwide, then leave it as "All Locations".
- Select the language of your target audience.
- Click on "Get Ideas".
- You'll see two tabs – "Ad group ideas" and "Keyword ideas". Look into both of them for keywords that are relevant to you and within the 1,000 – 10,000 monthly searches range. Save your desired keywords with their search volume in a new spreadsheet document.
- Select only one keyword you intend to focus on today. You'll save time if you get the work done now rather than reading it again later – but suit yourself.

READING

Now for the fun part. Open up Google and search the keyword you chose to focus on today… let's say, "How to make money" and read the first 10 blog post results you find on that topic – those will be the most popular, since they're the top results. Ensure they are blog posts/articles. If you don't have time to read them at the moment, then just save them for later. But you need to read them all so you can create a post better than all of them – in order to build links (no one is going to share a mediocre post).

Important note: "how to make money" has 301,000 monthly searches worldwide, so it's a bad target, but this is just for illustration. (It must be between 1,000 and 10,000 for a small startup).

Now you have a list of the top 10 articles that rank for your target keyword.

Take out your notebook and while you're going through each point (within an article), you need to ask yourself 5 questions:

• Can I go deeper on this specific point?
• Can I provide more or better examples?
• Can I make it better by adding some visuals such as screen shots and info graphics?
• Are there any missing points that I can add?
• Is the post too boring? Can I write it with more emotion? (Using the empathetic opening and motivational ending you learnt previously from the guest blogging section).

Do that with all 10 posts and make sure you spend enough time answering all 5 questions for each point. For example, if you're reading a post on "5 Ways to Make Money Online", you should answer those 5 questions on each single "Way" the article talks about... that's 25 questions in total.

What I like to do as well is, go to Quora.com, search for my keyword "How to Make Money" and read the top answers to get more ideas. But, this is optional.

WRITING

This is the part where you smash every single one of those 10 popular posts by writing the ultimate winner. You need to create the most in-depth blog post ever! You can refer to the tips I talked about previously in the guest blogging section if you have a problem with writing.

OUTREACH

Now that you're done writing, you need to promote it. Since, it's the best post on the topic, the chances of getting an influencer to share it, likely.

Back in the day, we used to head over to Topsy.com, search for influential people that shared one of those 10 posts (you just read) and message every single one of them with the news that you've written something better than what they shared in the past... then ask them to share it. Some would share, some would ignore.

But, topsy.com doesn't exist anymore!

What do you do?

You use Buzzsumo!

Hopefully, you haven't cancelled your free trial yet. If you have, then just sign up for another free trial using a different email.

Once you've done that, you're going to search for the people that shared the existing top 10 articles. Like this:

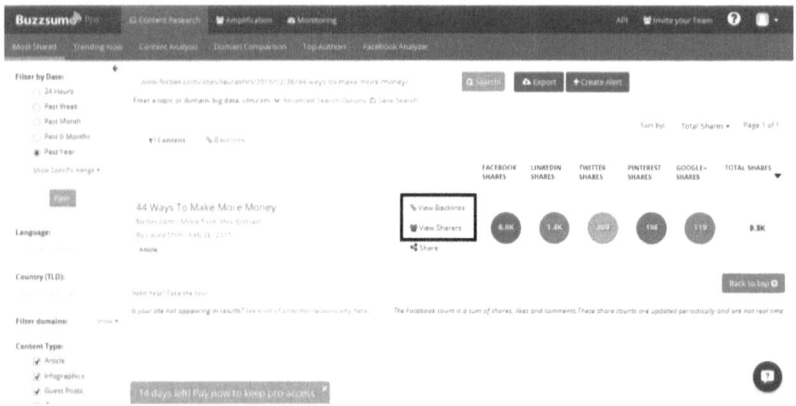

The goal is to find people who shared it on twitter. For this article, there are 809 sharers for twitter. Can you see the "View Sharers" and "View Backlinks" buttons in the middle of the screen? We're going to use them both, since your ranking will depend on both (links and shares).

Let's start with sharing: click the "View Sharers" button and you should get a list of sharers. You need to filter the results to include only "Influencers" and "Bloggers" (you can refine it more with location if you need to)… like this:

Filter by Type:

- ☑ Bloggers
- ☑ Influencers
- ☐ Companies
- ☐ Journalists
- ☐ Regular People

- ☐ Ignore Broadcasters

Location:

E.g city or country

Filter

Reset Filters

The influencers you want to reach out to should have at least 1,000 followers and a high "average retweets". This shows how engaged the audience is.

Now go to each influencer's twitter profile and see if they have their own website/blog. If they do, then go to their website and send them an email or message through the contact form on their website. If they don't link to any website in their profile, move onto the next influencer.

But what if they have a website/blog but don't mention any contact details? How do you contact them then?

Look for their email using Pipl.com!

You'll need to guess what their email is and Pipl.com will bring up one of their social media profiles if it's correct.

Let's say we're looking for my email;

We'll try the link I currently have in twitter which is zakmustapha.com and try adding some name and the @ symbol... in this format:

Name@zakmustapha.com

Now let's try some names...

zak@zakmustapha.com... Nope

zakmustapha@zakmustapha.com.... Nope

me@zakmustapha.com... Yep

As you can see, it pulled out the results from my Gravatar profile.

Another alternative to pipl.com is emailhunter.co that works pretty much the same way.

Anyway, save each influencers email in a spreadsheet document and once you're done, it's time to message them!

I hate templates so I'm not going to include one in this book... but all you should try to say is, that you want to give the person a "heads up" about your new ultimate blog post. Then paste the link for your article and wait for them to share it. If they share it, make sure you thank them.

Now that we're done with getting shares for our article, let's build some backlinks!

Go back to your Buzzsumo results and this time, click "View Backlinks". You'll see a list of websites that linked to the article, but this one is a bit tricky.

You need to aim for resources – articles that just link to other articles like this one:

Links We Love: 44 Ways to Make More Money
creditsesame.com - More from this domain
By Credit Sesame - Mar 2, 2015
Article

View Sharers
Share

Usually, they are really long posts like "100 resources for learning code" or anything to that nature.

Anyway, save a list of potential blogs that are likely to link to your blog post too. Once you're done, it's time to message them about your new article that may be a good addition to their existing list.

Begin your message by telling them how much you enjoyed their resource article and that you shared it. Then tell them that you've written an article yourself that may be a perfect addition to their resource article. Of course, don't forget to include your URL and also the URL for the resource list you wish to be included on.

Follow up in a week or two... if you get no replies after a few follow ups, then just leave them alone.

Congratulations, you've just written an awesome blog post, got it shared by influencers, got links from popular resource lists and most importantly, written about a topic that has a high search volume keyword!

You should hopefully see your post climbing up the Google ranks. If it doesn't, don't give up. Write another one. A good rule of thumb is to publish one of these monster articles at least, once a month.

Undefeated Marketing Secret #48: Write outstanding content that influencers and experts would love to share.

5
ONLINE MARKETING

Although a lot of the things we have covered in this book are branches of online marketing, I put this one separate due to their somewhat "general" nature.

49.   Trying to Maximize Web Visitors

So, you have a website, opt-in forms and content to attract more visitors to your website – that's good. But, what are web views or web visitors going to do for you?

I've seen many people who keep asking me how they can increase their website traffic. It's a really good question, but what's more important is how you convert website traffic. Because if you can't convert traffic, then traffic is useless.

Over 70% of visitors that come to your website will never come back! If you don't convert them the first time, then they are gone forever! [11]

So the question should be; how do I convert my website visitors?

The answer.... Go to the Conversion Marketing chapter.

In regards to increasing traffic... I've already covered that throughout the book, but I'll add on it... with a plan:

First, you need to know that there are two sources of traffic.... Paid and organic.

- Paid – Social media ads and other PPC (pay per click) methods of advertising.
- Organic – Guest blogging, social media, press release, podcasting, email, videos etc.
-

So, what I would do for traffic is this:

- Guest blog on a few popular blogs every month – The more, the better (assuming the blogs are sending you a good amount of traffic). I would link to a landing page with a special offer (such as an eBook) rather than my websites homepage – that way, I can get more subscribers. If I have time, I will actually create a personalized incentive just for the blog's readers whenever possible.

- I will spend around $50 on Facebook ADs and $50 on Twitter to build a small fan base to start with. $50 should get you over a thousand fans (but results are not typical). Since posting on an empty social account is... useless!

- Post bite sized content on social media for the purpose of entertaining people and not to sell them anything – I like to start with Instagram, Facebook and Twitter – LinkedIn as well, but you don't need to post several times a day on LinkedIn, so I just post links to helpful content from time to time. It all depends on your business. The important thing is to dedicate yourself to building an engaged fan base on at least, one social platform.

- While waiting for popular blogs to publish my articles, I start to write content for my blog in this time – incorporating the simple SEO tactics and including content upgrades in each post – as mentioned previously.

- Once I publish my article on my own blog, I will send an email to my subscribers and tell them to check it out – since subscribers do make up a large part of the traffic you get.

- If I have more money to spend on ADs, I would advertise my incentive (eBook or whatever) using Facebook ADs (or LinkedIn ADs if you're B2B) which will send social media users to my landing page that has the incentive. This way, I can build my email list faster. However, this doesn't replace guest blogging or the other methods of obtaining organic traffic.

That's pretty much it. There are other ways to obtain traffic like Google AdWords, interviewing influencers and guest podcasting, which you could do as well. In fact, if guest podcasting is also a good strategy but you need to find podcasts that interview people like you, I find it more beneficial for book authors.

Anyway, that's my answer. But, most importantly, is your website converting visitors? What are your conversion rates like? Keep improving. The higher your conversion rates, the less traffic you'll need.

Action Plan

Focus on converting traffic and not just getting it.

> **Undefeated Marketing Secret #49: Your traffic is useless if you can't convert it.**

50. Relying Only on Social Media for Promotion

The typical entrepreneur of today will use only social media for promoting articles and products. It's a good tactic and some businesses have made millions of dollars through social media especially on Instagram... but it is also very limiting to your true potential. You can do more! Here are a few ways (some we've already covered):

- Email Marketing

- Snail Mail
- Press Releases
- Influencer Marketing
- Word-of-mouth/referral marketing
- Guest Podcasting
- Paper advertising
- Directory Listing
- Flyers
- Seminars/Webinars
- Event marketing
- Much more

Action Plan

Promote via these popularly ignored marketing methods and you'll not only extend your reach, but you'll reach customers that your competitors never have – because, although a lot of the population is on social media, not all of them are and even those who are don't always respond to promotions on social media.

> **Undefeated Marketing Secret #50: Promote where the competition doesn't.**

51. Not Using Pictures

Researchers at Victoria University of Wellington in New Zealand found out that people will believe you if you put a picture, sometimes, even if it's a lie.[12]
When you want to describe an object, it's difficult to imagine it. But, when you add an image to it, it becomes

easier to comprehend and believe. Even an unrelated image next to a claim makes it more believable. Of course, you shouldn't lie.

Action Plan

Use images to strengthen your claims.

> *Undefeated Marketing Secret #51: Power up your claims with pictures.*

52. Not Measuring Results

Just because I told you Facebook ADs worked for me, doesn't mean they will work for you. Maybe LinkedIn ADs work better for you, but bad for me. It all depends on the industry you're in. Same goes for opt-in form types, web design and everything else.

Always measure your return on investment. If you were to invest $50 on Facebook ADs to gain traffic for your website and you got 36 subscribers from the AD, it means you paid $1.39 per subscriber. Is that a success for you? Well, that depends on how much each subscriber is worth to your business (remember value ladder #12).

It all depends on your ROI. Whatever has a positive ROI, do more of it. If not, then try something else. Most importantly, whatever actions you decide to take, make sure they are based on hard data and not assumptions and personal preference.

Action Plan

Measure results and then decide whether you should continue, stop or make some changes.

> **Undefeated Marketing Secret #52: Make decisions based on hard proof and you'll never go wrong.**

53. Measuring Vanity Metrics

Since we've talked about measuring results, I had to bring this up. Because a lot of startup entrepreneurs focus on metrics that don't even matter. They measure stuff that makes no difference on their bottom line. In other words, they focus on vanity (useless) metrics.

Things such as, number of website visitors instead of email subscribers. Or they measure how many people sign up for their software product but ignore how many actually pay or use it regularly. Or they focus on the number of people that opened up their email and ignore the number of people who actually clicked the link inside the email. I can go on all day.

The point I'm trying to highlight is this; make sure you're focusing on the important metrics that get you closer to your goals. You want, people to buy your products? You measure sales– focus on actionable metrics (metrics you can make use of).

Action Plan

Measure actionable metrics and don't be deceived by vanity metrics that make no difference to your bottom line. Take time to identify your two most important metrics – then work on improving them.

> *Undefeated Marketing Secret #53: Ignore vanity metrics.*

54. Building on Moving Foundations

Gaining traffic from social media and search engines is useful and something every business must do. However, if it's the only source of traffic you have, then you're in serious danger. Depending solely on these methods is like building a house on a moving, unstable foundation such as a ship.

The reason behind that is that search engines and social platforms update their algorithms regularly. You never know what sudden changes they'll make. A lot of business owners in the past depended only on Google and social media for traffic and when the algorithms were updated, many small business owners took a hit – their traffic dropped down to almost zero overnight. You don't want that to happen to you. And the best way to avoid is... Don't depend on it.

Action Plan

Don't depend ONLY on social media and Google for your traffic. Utilize all the other sources of traffic as well, at least that way, if you ever get affected by their updates, it won't be as bad. You don't own your social media accounts nor do you own your Google ranking but you do own a website.

Undefeated Marketing Secret #54: Have multiple streams of traffic.

---

55. Overpromising & Under Delivering

I know you're probably young and just starting out, you want to impress the customers, there's too much competition so you make a huge promise to your customer, but then you realize you can't deliver what you just promised…Oops…

So what do you do now? Don't do it again! Apologize and refund their money back.

What's worse, most people who overpromise don't do it on purpose. They believe they really can deliver what they promised, but once they fail, they realize they just overpromised.

How do you solve such a problem?

You under promise, then surprise them by over delivering.

Here's an example: let's say you're a writer and someone hires you to write a 1,500 word article for $150 to be submitted in 7 days. When you deliver the project, you give your client a 2,000 word article instead. Your client will be thrilled to get more than what they paid for.

However, in the beginning, you should have accounted the time and costs it would take for a 2,000 word article yet, promised 1,500 to be safe. That way, you'll be sure not to disappoint any customers.

Action Plan

Always under promise and over deliver. Never promise equal or more than you can do.

> *Undefeated Marketing Secret #55: Under promise then surprise with more.*

6
SOCIAL MEDIA MARKETING

Social media marketing is where everyone goes to do their marketing these days. It's also one of the hardest to do if you don't know what you're doing.

56. Expecting a Fixed Guide for Social Media

I'm sorry to burst your bubble, but there is no such thing as a solid social media guide that works for everyone. However, you will find different strategies that have worked for other companies in the past that may possibly work for you as well. I have included a list of several strategies that some businesses implement in the bonus material.

However, there are basic principles to follow when marketing on social media that I'll cover.

Action Plan

- Don't ask (for a sale) before you've entertained your fans several times.
- Try to write as little as possible.
- Create sharable content i.e. funny stuff people can relate to.
- Always post an image (where possible).
- Be consistent (don't disappear for too long).
- Measure results and post more of what your fans like.

Undefeated Marketing Secret #56: Social media is an ever-changing game.

57. Increasing the Number of Fans Through Following and Unfollowing

Have you seen it? These accounts that follow and then unfollow, again and again? Don't they just annoy you with notifications all the time?

Following in return for a follow is the cheapest tactic ever. A lot of those who will follow you back will only do it because they feel bad if they didn't. The worst part is, people will remember that you followed and unfollowed them, which is bad reputation for your brand.

Action Plan

Don't follow and unfollow. You can share other people's content, like other people's content, comment on other people's content, use hashtags and purchase ADs.

> *Undefeated Marketing Secret #57: Following and unfollowing is the cheapest tactic ever.*

58. Afraid of Sharing Old Timeless Content

Just because you shared something 5 months ago, doesn't mean you can't share it again to your followers. If it was relevant back then, then it should be relevant today, unless it's a timely piece of content, of course.

Action Plan

Share timeless content to your followers. You worked hard on it and it was helpful to your old fans several months ago. Don't forget to show it to your new fans.

Undefeated Marketing Secret #58: Timeless content can be shared more than once.

---

59. Not Understanding How The Platform's Algorithm Works

If you know how the algorithm works, you will understand how to get on people's news feed and get more engagement for your posts. It's all about getting on the news feed. Because if you don't make it in people's news feed, they won't be able to see it and if they can't see, they can't engage with it.

Obviously, I'm not going to start telling you about how the algorithms of each social media platform works – that would be silly – not to forget, almost impossible since they always update them.

So instead, I'm going to give you simple straightforward advice. If you post quality content that a user likes right now, you will make it into their news feed in the future. Remember that small drop down menu you get on each news feed update on Facebook? You know... the one that gives you the option to hide what you don't like. It looks something like this:

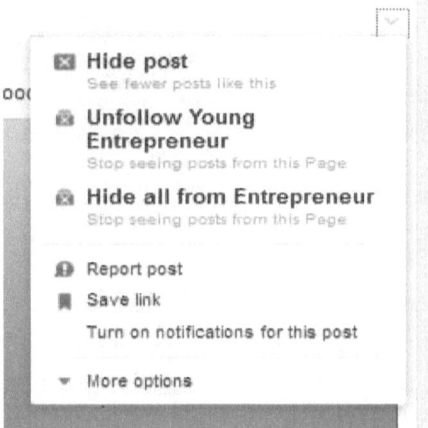

YEAH, THAT ONE! Can you see what it says under "Hide post"? It says, "See fewer posts like this" and that tells the Facebook algorithm that I don't want to see posts from this business/user. Now imagine all you did was post sales and promotions? Users will likely click on "Hide all from Business name" and stop seeing everything you post!

And that is why you should NEVER, EVER post stuff users don't want to see in the first place.

But, it brings up a question.... What do users want to see? Well, you can start off by asking yourself, why do users go to social media in the first place?

Chat with friends, see the latest news, entertainment, funny stuff etc.

They don't go on social media to buy stuff. No one ever said "hey I wanna do some shopping, let me open up Facebook!" It doesn't work that way.

Your content must be interesting to the user. Post what everyone else is posting. Be a human and humanize your brand.

Go ahead and post memes, latest sports game scores, and all the other stuff your fans do. This applies not only for Facebook, but pretty much every social media platform works in a similar way. The more hearts, likes, shares, retweets, reposts and comments you get, the higher the algorithm pushes you up people's news feed.

Action Plan

Follow the latest news on social media algorithm changes so you can understand how to get your content seen by more users. It may sound boring to read about algorithm updates, but it would do you good in the long run. Don't forget, that most people don't do this, so you'll have an unfair advantage over them – because you know what they don't know.

Open up Google and type "[social media platform] latest algorithm update" for whatever site you want to know about. Go through the search results and look for the latest one available, then read it and make sure you understand what it means.

Find out what people want to see by asking yourself, "What do people come to do on [social media platform]?" Once you've figured the type of content they like to see, post more of it.

Undefeated Marketing Secret #59: Stay up to date with the latest algorithm updates so you know how to get more users to see your content.

---

60. Not Posting Regularly

Admit it. You've done it before. We all do it. We have a product we need to sell, so we start posting up on social media hoping to make a sale. But, it doesn't happen that way. Social media isn't for making a quick sale. Social media is a long term game and posting needs to be done regularly.

Action Plan

Post bite-sized content regularly... something that will give people a laugh or a smile or any sort of emotion. Keep doing it continuously. Take Oreo's social media accounts as an example; they do it well... learn from them. (I have included in the bonus material, a list of social media accounts you should learn from for inspiration. Think of it as your social media swipe file).

> **Undefeated Marketing Secret #60: Take mini steps regularly on social media.**

61. Sending Your Message across the Wrong Channels

Where does your ideal customer hang out?
Are they other businesses? Women? Celebrities? Old people? Teenagers?

Each platform is has different users:
- LinkedIn is mainly for B2B
- Instagram users are mostly between ages 18 - 30
- Pinterest has over 85% female users
- Facebook has almost everyone
- Twitter users are between ages 18 - 45

The above data are just averages for the year 2015 and may change in the future.

Action Plan

Make sure you send the right message to the right audience. When you make a joke or post a funny picture, keep in mind the age of your fans. You don't want to post an 18-year old joke to 40-year olds.

> **Undefeated Marketing Secret #61: Know your fans on each social platform – they are not always the same.**

62. Responding to internet trolls

Trolls are everywhere now. They hide behind fake names and pictures and harass you online. There two types of trolls:
- Hater Troll
- Joker Troll

The hater troll is the one who just insults your brand and tries to bring down your reputation. He's just trying to pick a fight.

The Joker troll will make fun of your brand and write stupid comments under your posts.

Both of them will try their best to mess with your business. Responding to them only makes things worse. When you respond to them, they'll start playing their game with you. If you ignore them, then they may just move on to someone who will play their game.

However, if they don't stop trolling your brand, you could easily block them and they'll never see you again (unless they create a new account).

Action Plan

Ignore and block trolls – don't waste your time with trolls, you have a business to run.

> **Undefeated Marketing Secret #62: Ignore and block trolls.**

63. Sharing Brags and Good Words from Customers

You've seen it, haven't you? Especially on Twitter. They do it a lot. Big brands will retweet a kind words that came from their customer, just to show the world that people love them. It's lame and doesn't amuse your fans. Why would they engage with a brag about your brand?

Action Plan

Post something worth sharing – something funny or interesting – anything worth sharing.

64. Making Stupid Offensive Jokes and Speaking About Sensitive Topics

I don't even need to talk about this.

Action Plan

Don't talk crap. Don't make jokes on serious hashtags and vice versa.

65. Sharing the Same Stuff on All Social Media Platforms

Each social media platform is unique – therefore, the content must be unique. Don't share the same exact picture on every single one of your platforms at the same time.

An Instagram square shaped photo isn't suitable for Twitter that has horizontal rectangle shaped photos. A vertical rectangular photo from Pinterest isn't suitable for Instagram, etc.

Action Plan

Don't share the exact same picture on all platforms at the same time - and never share what doesn't fit another platform e.g. Instagram picture on Twitter.

> **Undefeated Marketing Secret #65: Share different content on different platforms – each platform has its own content requirements.**

66. Writing too Much

There are now over 2 billion social media users and 77% is mobile.[14] The number of people that use their mobile phones for social media has surpassed desktop users. Now everyone runs around in the street looking at their phones instead of the road.

But, what does this all mean to you?

It means you need to post your content for mobile users because they are the majority.

I see a lot of posts on Facebook, Instagram and Pinterest writing a full essay as a caption or status update. Somehow, they must have thought that people would actually read it while on the run. What were they thinking?

Everyone just scrolls down. Likes the picture, maybe reads a sentence or two and that's it. Oh yeah, did I mention that you need a picture for each post? (Except for twitter)

Action Plan

Create mobile friendly content. That means put an eye catching photo and a short caption. You don't need to give them a load of content to consume; keep it small.

> **Undefeated Marketing Secret #66: Bite-sized content is like a tasty snack for your fans – people love snacks. It makes them want more.**

67. Blaming Yourself for Follower Loss

Unless you've posted something stupid, don't blame yourself for losing followers. Many people follow and unfollow other accounts so they can grow their own followers. It's nothing personal, they're just being cheap.

Action Plan

Don't blame yourself for losing followers unless you posted something stupid, or you've spammed your followers too much. If it was because of something wrong from your part, then fix it and learn from it. Getting emotional about it won't help.

> **Undefeated Marketing Secret #67: Learn from your social mistake and move on – no emotions.**

68. Bad Mouthing Competition

Talking bad about your competition makes YOU look bad. It shows that your brand has nothing to talk about other than its competitors in an attempt to look good in front of your fans. Your fans are already your fans. Research shows that bad traits you attribute to others will reflect back to you. It's called spontaneous trait transference. [13] The next time you talk ill about someone, remember that it reflects back on you.

Action Plan

Don't bad mouth anyone. Focus on your startup. No time to waste on others.

> **Undefeated Marketing Secret #68: Be good mouthed with competitors – online and offline.**

69. Not Putting Logos on Images

It's nice to see you've taken some effort to have a picture on your post, but you need to put your logo on it. For two reasons:

One, so people know straight away who posted it without having to look at the little profile picture.

Two, in case anyone decides to share it; you'll get added exposure because they'll see your logo on the shared image.

Here's an example from Foolishness File:

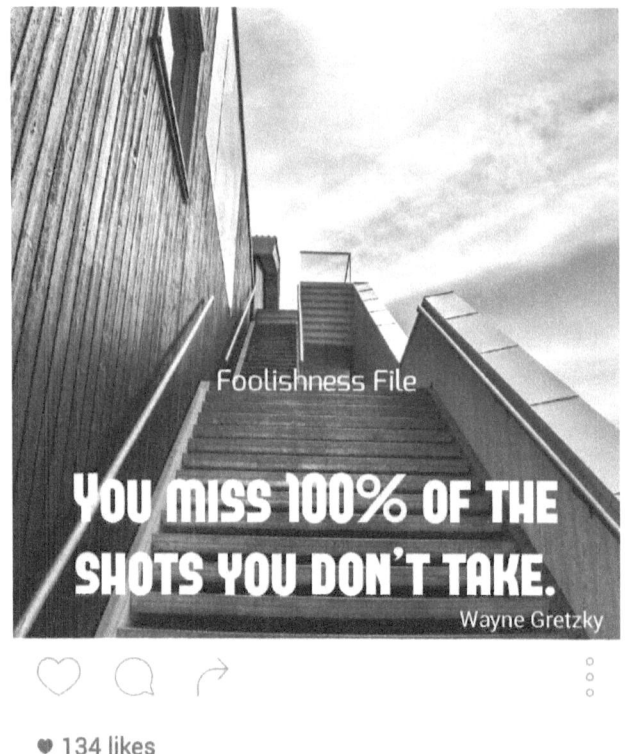

Foolishness File

YOU MISS 100% OF THE SHOTS YOU DON'T TAKE.
Wayne Gretzky

♥ 134 likes

foolishnessfile Take your shots.

Here's another example from Foundr Magazine…

THE FACT THAT YOU'RE NOT WHERE YOU WANT TO BE YET SHOULD BE ENOUGH MOTIVATION

found

♡ ○ ↱

♥ 5,913 likes

foundrmagazine Here's your reminder... Double tap
if you are with us!

Action Plan

Put your logo on all your images.

> *Undefeated Marketing Secret #69: Sign your content with
> your unique logo.*

70. Not Respecting Social Media as an Independent Platform

Numerous marketers treat social media as a distribution channel for new products and articles. But, it's not. Social media is where people go to connect with friends, families and entertain themselves when they are bored. The last thing they want to see is a 50% spring sale on your leather jackets.

Stop treating social media as a junk yard for your promotions. Post the type of content a real human would post, not a salesy business. Here's an example of what you should post on Facebook:

 **Audi USA**
20 hrs

Perk of growing up: Trading out your sled for an #AudiA6. #quattro
audi.us/A6

Like   Comment   Share

Every Audi fan appreciates a beautiful car in the snow. This photo received over 14 thousand likes and over 450 shares in just 20 hours... but Audi does have 9 million fans... so you won't get the same results. However, look at how simple the post is... one line of text and a link to the cars landing page... no hard selling... just a beautiful car and a bit of text.

Here's an example of a clever and somewhat funny tweet by Nutella...

 **Nutella** ✅
@NutellaUSA    ✿ ⊱ Follow

How do you become a lifetime fan of Nutella®?
Try it once.

Nutella truly knows its fans and shows them that it not only understands them but also has a sense of humor.

Here's an example of an excellent Instagram post:

♥ 87,091 likes

bmw Is it still considered a pitstop if the only landmark you're stopping to admire is your very own classic #BMW?

That post by BMW is just an awesome classic. It fits perfectly into the Instagram theme. People come to Instagram to see beautiful pictures... and this one blends a classic BMW car with beautiful scenery. The copy is short too... perfect for mobile.

By the way, before finding these amazing posts, I had to go through a lot of terrible ones that I found on billion dollar brands! I told you their size means nothing. You can bet the HR team that hired the social media marketing team didn't have a clue about marketing – but you do! Don't lose hope, you're getting there.

Action Plan

Post independent content on each social platform – don't do too many cross promotions. When you want to post something on Facebook, you make it for Facebook, and post it on Facebook for your audience on Facebook. When you want to post on Instagram, you make a picture for Instagram and post it there for the audience on Instagram, etc.

Undefeated Marketing Secret #70: Independent platforms deserve independent content.

---

71. Intruding People's Social Feed

How do you intrude into someone's social life?

Someone is sitting with their friends, talking about tonight's game. As they are laughing because of some baseball joke one of them made, you (the salesperson) interrupt them and ask them if they would be interested in buying handmade watches.

What do you think happens now?

Well, one of them will reply, "no thanks" and then they'll just get on with their conversation.

Why did they tell you to get lost in a nice way?

Simply because you were intruding!

You barged into the conversation they were having and changed the topic.

But, this was a face to face experience. What about social media? Great question... EXACTLY the same! No difference between them. People are people – online and face-to-face – it doesn't change a thing!

If everyone is talking about the game, then YOU talk about the game. Don't post a sales picture of your watch, it's going to be intruding to the common theme of that day and that platform, which would likely be full of pictures related to baseball.

For some reason, people think they can just barge in and sell their stuff anywhere and anytime. Actually, they can, sometimes, if they don't intrude.

However, it needs to be done in a smart way. Instead of posting a watch, with overlaying "50% OFF" script on top, you should put something related to the game.

Perhaps a picture of a baseball cap, scarf, popcorn and whatever else fans take with them along with the watch you want to sell. Then you could say something like: "Got your game gear ready?"

It's a nice way to show that your product fits into whatever is going on and isn't an intruder. It also humanizes your brand and lets people know that you are aware of what's happening in the world.

Then an hour before the game, you could put another picture of your watch and have an overlaying script saying something like, "Tick Tock, It's almost time!" Then in the caption you could say, "Don't forget... game starts in an hour."

You'll likely gain a few followers just from a post like that. You'll become like a friend, reminding them not to forget to do the stuff they enjoy in their life. It not only humanizes you, it also makes you a fun brand.

So yeah, that's how you do it without being an intruder.

Action Plan

Be relevant to whatever is happening. Don't intrude. Be entertaining.

Undefeated Marketing Secret #71: Become people's entertainment.

---

72. Not Trying Out New Platforms

Don't limit yourself to just Facebook, Twitter, Instagram, Pinterest and all the other popular social media platforms. Try different social platforms even if they are small – they'll be easier to dominate.

The first brands on Instagram have massive of followings now. They have built profitable companies out of Instagram while everyone else was still doing their old stuff... a lot of these small timers were building businesses out of it. Then all the big companies joined and they found all the little kids had taken over. There was this guy who owned @entrepreneur on Instagram before Entrepreneur Magazine owned it – it had a 5-figure price tag. I would have sold it for 6!

Anyway, when everyone starts jumping onto a social media platform, it will be too late. Obviously, it doesn't mean you don't jump on it too, it just means it will be harder to dominate it.

An example of some new/underrated platforms would be Periscope, Quora and possibly Hyper.

Action Plan

Be open to exploring other social media platforms other than the popular ones.

> *Undefeated Marketing Secret #72: Dominating one small platform is better than being a nobody everywhere.*

7
EMAIL MARKETING

This Email Marketing chapter is rather short because, it's pretty much similar to the content marketing/copywriting and social media stuff you just learnt previously – you're just having a conversation with your fans and offering them great content. In fact, a good rule of thumb is to send 80% entertainment and 20% useful content, because people don't want to be bombarded with too much information all at once, give it to them in bite sizes. Email them like you'd email a friend.

73. Blaming Yourself for Subscriber Loss

You will lose subscribers. Sometimes, it will be your fault and sometimes, it won't. Just accept it, people will lose interest or want to organize their inbox.

I sometimes unsubscribe to newsletters that are interesting to me because I don't have time for them. My work is more important than getting 70 newsletters every day. So, don't take it personal when someone unsubscribes.

On the other hand, if you see a high unsubscription rate right after something you've sent, then there could be a good reason behind it. Did you offend someone? Did you say something stupid? Did you send them multiple emails a day?

Figure out what it is and don't repeat it.

Since we're on the topic... how often should you email subscribers?

It depends, the maximum is once a day (yes, once every single day) and the minimum is once a month. Just make sure your emails are exciting and useful.

Action Plan

Figure out why people unsubscribed but don't overthink it and get emotionally affected by it. You're there to learn why they unsubscribed so you can get better.

Undefeated Marketing Secret #73: Don't worry about unsubscriptions. Learn!

---

74. Afraid of Following up Because You Don't Want to be Annoying

Why don't people reply the first time?
- It could be because they're busy
- They get too many emails
- They decide to respond later but then forget
- They don't want to reply/not interested in what you have to offer

Out of all those four possibilities, only the last person could possibly find you annoying. But, what if the person happened to be one of the other three?

What does it matter anyway?

The worst that will happen is you'll get….nothing. No reply. Silence. That's all.

Okay, maybe you'll get someone who tells you, "get lost", but that fine… it's part of the game. If you can't handle someone ignoring you or telling you to leave them alone, then how are you going to survive the real difficulties in business?

Action Plan

Send around four follow ups and distance them a week or two apart for whenever you need someone to respond.

> **Undefeated Marketing Secret #74: Always follow up – don't be afraid.**

75. Writing Long Subject Lines

There's not enough space. If you write really long subject lines, they'll be covered with ellipsis (the 3 dots).
Try to keep it as short as possible. Use questions too. People have been taught since they were young to answer when people ask them questions – so you're likely to get a response.
Another thing to remember is that people usually get several emails a day and they don't have time to read a 15-word subject line.

Action Plan

Keep your subject lines short and to the point. Intrigue the subscriber with powerful copy.

> **Undefeated Marketing Secret #75: Long subject lines are weak and fluffy.**

76. Ignoring Spam Emails

What do people usually do with spam emails? Delete them right?
As a writer of email subject lines, you need to know how to avoid sounding spammy – so what should you do?
Save Spam. Read Spam!

Action Plan

Read the spam headlines and analyze their structure so you can avoid writing subject lines that sound spammy at all costs – your junk folder is the best place to learn how you shouldn't write an email. The email filter throws them in the junk folder for a reason (hint: their spammy words).

> *Undefeated Marketing Secret #76: Junk folders help you learn what to avoid.*

77. Shouting or Whispering

Don't write all caps or all lower case in a subject line – it just looks bad. Here, have a look for yourself:
Subject: DOWNLOAD THE SPECIAL BONUS TODAY
Subject: download the special bonus today
Subject: Download the Special Bonus Today
Which one looks better? The last one, of course. It's balanced and easy on the eye... it's what you're used to seeing on magazines, newspapers and online.

Action Plan

Type the first letters in capital and the rest in lower case to achieve a balanced subject line.

> *Undefeated Marketing Secret #77: Balanced subject lines appear less spammy and are easy to read.*

78. Being Too Formal

Every once in a while, include your subscribers name in the subject line. When someone sees their name in the subject line, it feels personal, they just have to open it because it addresses them personally. Someone is calling them and they have to answer that call.

Your email marketing service should have a personalization field to include people's first name – use it. However, don't do it too often, otherwise, they'll just get used to it. A lot of marketers do it so many times they just ruin it for everybody. Don't be that marketer!

Action Plan

Put their first name in the subject line every once in a while.

> **Undefeated Marketing Secret #78: Call them by their first name in the subject line... sometimes.**

79. Not Delivering The Subject's Promise

How many times have you seen an intriguing subject line, open the email and be totally disappointed? I hate that too. Everyone hates a liar.

Action Plan

Write a subject line that is relevant to the message.

> *Undefeated Marketing Secret #79: Lying will destroy your credibility with subscribers.*

80. Not Testing

It's marketing. You never know what will work and what won't. You could follow every rule in the book and yet fail, or break every single law of marketing and get outstanding results. You just never know… it's marketing! Whenever you write subject lines, test them. Send one subject line to half of your subscribers and another one to the other half. Then after a few days, check the open rates. You'll learn a lot by knowing which subject lines work better than others.

Action Plan

Test subject lines to see which ones your subscribers respond to the best.

> *Undefeated Marketing Secret #80: Testing teaches you more than theory.*

8
WORD-OF-MOUTH
MARKETING

The best companies grow through word-of-mouth. Either face-to-face or online. Businesses such as DropBox, Facebook and all the other huge companies of today. The best part about it is that the costs for word-of-mouth (or referral) marketing is extremely low – you can almost say it's free. In fact, if most businesses such as Instagram or Facebook paid for their traffic, they would have ran out of money or stayed small.

81. Having No System

Most businesses generate a chunk of their revenues from referrals. From your local bakery to the hairdresser down the street, they depend on referrals. But, surprisingly, they don't have any system for referrals, instead, they just let it happen.

But, I understand why they do that. One, they didn't think they needed a system for getting referrals. Two, they are scared to be seen as desperate, needy, annoying or that they'll ruin the relationship with their customer.

The first problem is already solved for you, because now, you know you need a system (if you didn't know before). The second problem can be fixed with a change of mindset. You're not being desperate, needy and annoying, you just want to help more people and provide them high value products/services.

So how do you build this system I talk about?

- Treat your employees exceptionally well, so they can do the same to the customer – you're their leader and role model.

- Put your employees through training – Zappos put their employees through 4 weeks customer-focused training and then offers to pay them for the work they did, plus a $2,000 bonus to quit the job – to test whether the employee is customer focused or money focused. It's an investment that has paid off substantially since Zappos grew by word-of-mouth.[15]

- Ask your customers if they know anyone who you could help.

- Create events (customers usually bring friends with them, so you'll get access to those new people).
- The same way you have a buyer persona, create an employee persona so you can target the right employees that fit your culture.
- Mention that you reward referrals on all you leaflets, websites, brochures and emails etc.
- Give current customers discount vouchers that they should give to a friend and they themselves earn a discount when their friend uses the discount voucher.
- Be trustworthy in everything you do (i.e. advertisements) – people don't refer businesses/products they don't trust.
- Make your expectations clear to employees and customers that you expect them to generate referrals.
- Create a referral community.
- Solve customer problems fast – put off the fire whilst it's still small.
- Educate the customer with impressive content (people refer experts).

Putting a referral system is an investment that will pay for itself multiple times. It's the best investment you'll make. But, you may need to charge higher prices to sustain such a system. Being the number 1 cheapest store and the best in customer service isn't sustainable.

Oh yeah, and in case you're wondering when you should ask for a referral, you should ask for a referral while you're delivering a great product/service and after you've done delivered it... yeah I know, it wasn't that hard, but you're assured after I've said it.

Action Plan

Start building your referral system – it's a continuous process. (I have included an ultimate list of ideas to help build your system in the bonus material).

Undefeated Marketing Secret #81: Create a referral system.

---

82. Being a Copycat

Did you ever refer your local gas station? Of course not, it's boring, the same as every other gas station. Besides, what would a gas station owner do anyway to make his place exciting to people – it's just gas, right?

Wrong! You can do a lot to a gas station. First, they could dress their employees neatly, warmly welcome visitors, fill up people's tanks, and offer them a small gift such as a tissue box or a quick car clean or tire pressure check. You could also add a repair garage with the station and hire well informed engineers. That way, people will come to you not only for gas but also for car repairs.

If you do give a free tissue box with every full tank, people will be extra careful to fill up with you rather than a different gas station (as long as you're the only one giving away free tissue boxes).

People refer because it makes them look good in front of people. But, if your business is just the same boring business like everyone else, then there's no point for them to refer you... that will just ruin their reputation.

Action Plan

Be different. Be astonishing. Do the opposite. Ask yourself, "How can I get people to talk about my business?

> *Undefeated Marketing Secret #82: People talk about Mr. Opposite, make sure it's good.*

83. Having No Secrets

Don't tell people every single thing. Keep some secrets to create curiosity. Many (if not all) successful companies such as Coca Cola, Google and KFC have secrets. It's good for two reasons: One, competitors won't be able to copy you (since they don't know your ingredients, algorithms etc.). Two, people will be curious and therefore talk about it – you'll be the only business that offers a secretive good product – when you tell people that you have a secret, their curiosity will make them want to hunt down your secret. Don't give it to them, let them talk and snoop around – you'll get yourself some pretty good press releases and traffic.

Action Plan

Look for a secret that your product has, whether it is in the algorithm, ingredients, whatever. There has to be a secret – if there isn't, you make one.

> *Undefeated Marketing Secret #83: Secrets make you interesting.*

84. Not Changing and Innovating

Humans want new stuff. No one asks for old stuff (only in rare cases). When you buy a book, you want the latest edition. A phone, you want the new one. A car, you'll go for the latest model (unless you're into classics), the point is; people want new stuff.

If car companies, tech companies and all the other companies didn't get better constantly, people would lose interest in them. If the iPhone looked the same for all its years, less people would buy it. It makes sense; I don't even need to mention this. But, a lot companies even the ones that are not in tech, don't innovate, but should. Even a barbershop should innovate!

You could let people book their haircuts through some online App or on a website. Give them a TV to watch while waiting and getting the haircut. A hair wash, so they can just get on with their day without having to go home for a shower.... a car wash... Whatever... just innovate... those are just some suggestions. Stop being the same boring barbershop you've been for years.

If I see a barbershop that allows me book my preferred time, you can be sure I'll tell EVERYONE about it. I'll go there even if it costs me more, because let's face it, they are letting me chose my own time... so they deserve to get paid more.

Action Plan

Innovate and avoid being the same business you've been for the past few months or years. Launch new products, make current ones better, introduce a new service, etc.

> **Undefeated Marketing Secret #84:** *No one talks about old rusty businesses.*

85. Ignoring Customer's Perception

If customers perceive you as a prestigious brand, then you're prestigious. If the customers perceive you as a young trendy brand, then you're a young trendy brand. You know what I'm trying to say right? The customer's perception is the reality.

When you look at a Ferrero Roche chocolate, you feel luxury, when you pay for it, you feel like you've bought a superior chocolate, then as you unwrap the golden foil and take a bite through the nutty biscuit chocolate, it's the best moment in your life. As you can see, it didn't just stop with the packaging, the Ferrero did their best to make sure the perception was consistent throughout to give you a luxury experience.

Action Plan

Get your notebook out and write down the perception you want to convey. Then work towards it and always ask yourself if what you're doing is according to the perception you previously wrote down in your notebook.

Undefeated Marketing Secret #85: Consistency in customer perception is vital.

---

86. Taking Loyalty for Granted

If you see a customer coming to your place often, you don't just "take their order". You give them VIP treatment. He or she is a loyal customer and they didn't have to be. YET, they chose to be. So now, you have to treat them with royalty.

Many businesses will do their best to acquire new customers and prefer them to the current ones – because the current ones are used to coming here, anyway... he won't mind if I let him wait... he'll understand I'm trying to impress a new customer, right?

Turns out, new customer is just visiting town and old loyal customer left his local store just to come to you.

It does happen, it happened with me when I went for vacation in Lebanon, I would walk with my cousin to the juice place to have freshly made mixed fruit juice with cream on top. Even though there were many closer juice places nearby, we wanted the one located in the far end of the village because we just liked the place. Whenever I go to Lebanon, the owner knows, he's going to make enough money to pay bills for the next two month, because when my cousins and I order, we don't order large... we order an off-the-menu vase... In fact, let me show you a picture of it...

That's the one we have when we're not too hungry. There's a bigger one which is three times as large as those, but I won't show a picture of it... you'll think we're monsters.

Anyway, we ordered almost the same juice mix every day, it was crowded, no one took my order, I was invisible, no warm welcome, no nothing. We decided to come back later... so we went back and after 3 or 4 hours, the fruits finished.

I thought it was a one off... so we went again... and again... and again... then, my cousin told me that we should never go back there anymore... we didn't.

The problem was... his business was doing well... but it could have done A LOT better if he made a few changes. He could have expanded his place since there was plenty of space on both left and right sides of the place. By just counting the customers he got per hour, it didn't need a genius to figure out they could afford an expansion.

The other thing is, if you know you get a lot of new customers, at least, tell your loyal ones to come back in an hour or something. Don't just ignore them and let them come back every hour.

It wasn't just me and my cousin... in fact, I saw several regular faces come to his place... only to find out there's no stock left. His stock would finish all the time... he never had a surplus, never hired more employees, never expanded, never gave VIP treatment and gratitude to his loyal customers – he neglected them... want to know the worst part? He didn't listen to customers, because they would tell him... but he didn't care. Oh well, why be a multi-millionaire when you can just pay the bills, eh?

Action Plan

Show appreciation to loyal customers – they don't owe it to you.

Undefeated Marketing Secret #86: Treat loyalty with royalty.

---

87. Your Products Ain't Cool to Create a Network Effect

Your products are never going to spread unless they become a cool thing to have. It has to be trendy. Your product needs to make people feel like they are missing out or outdated if they don't buy your product. Just like what happens with the iPhone. People camp in front of the store just so they can get their hands on the latest iPhone – because it's cool, trendy and totally worth it!

But, your product doesn't need to appeal to everyone for it to spread, it could appeal to just a certain group. It can be anything trendy; the latest gadget, equipment, clothing etc.

Action Plan

Make your products cool through promoting it as a cool product, giving it a cool touch or design, be open to new ideas, be flexible and agile, don't micromanage employees, sell it to cool people, give it to the most popular people in schools so everyone else can follow them... celebrities etc.

Undefeated Marketing Secret #87: People want cool products from cool businesses.

---

88. Not Rewarding Referrers

When you get a referral from someone, what do most businesses do? Nothing. The best they'll do is say "thanks" and flash a smile. They won't be seeing much referrals after that though.

Businesses must give something in return for referrals. Referrers just sent you a paying customer! Reward them!

Action Plan

Give referrers discounts, free stuff… just create a reward program.

Undefeated Marketing Secret #88: Reward referrers.
---

89. Bad With Customer Service

Customer service doesn't belong to only the customer service employees… it belongs to everyone – everyone must know it. Let me tell you a story…

Two weeks ago (from writing this), my aunt and sister went to mall to fetch some stuff and decided to get some candy for the kids. As they walked into the candy shop, there was this guy giving out free candy to people. When he saw my aunt and her kids walking in, he didn't give them the free candy, but he gave everyone else.

It's not like he didn't see them. He did.

Anyway, my aunt walked to the aisle where they had the candy and the same guy who ignored them came and said, "you eat vegetarian, right?" (Since he knew Muslims don't have candy with pork gelatin) They said, "yes", and he explained that he didn't give them candy at the door because the candy he was giving wasn't vegetarian. And because they only ate vegetarian candy... he came to help them pick the right ones (even though the ingredients were visible). And he started talking and explaining the ingredients... what's good, what's bad... everything there's possibly to say about candy... he gave them FREE candy education.

Because of the employees helpfulness and emotional intelligence, my aunt didn't just buy a bit of candy... she bought A LOT.

... If it was me... I'd hire him. Or train my employees to be just as helpful. Not only was he helpful, he also knew "what was up."

Action Plan

Treat your customers as honorable guests, be courteous, answer all their questions, create a process for handling complaints and don't scare them away with strict policy – train and educate employees to become masters at customer service and customer educators.

> *Undefeated Marketing Secret #89: Serve and welcome customers as honored guests.*

90. Giving Customers What They Expect

If you give your customers what they expect from you, then you have failed.

If you order a pair of shoes online, you expect shoes. However, when you order a pair of shoes online, but get shoes AND a thank you card with a small gift with inside... "WOW" In fact, just a handwritten thank you note will make you say, "wow", maybe not as big as the first wow, but still a wow.

Action Plan

Wow the customer with something they never expected.

> **Undefeated Marketing Secret #90: Don't give the customer what they expect to receive.**

91. Being Only Transactional

So, we've talked about rewards, innovations, conveying a perception, showing gratitude to loyal customers and so on. But, there's something missing... community!

Take Starbucks as an example; they are not just a café; they are people's third place between home and work. People come to Starbucks not to just drink coffee but to sit on a comfy chair, surf the web, talk on the phone and just feel at home. Coffee is a by-product to accompany those things. That's been the mission of Starbucks all along... to become the third place between home and work.

Don't just make your business a place where people transact, make it a place they chose to be. Make it a third place like Starbucks!

Action Plan

If you have a brick and mortar business, then make your place feel like home, put chairs, coffee machines, snacks...maybe a billiard table too... you know.

> *Undefeated Marketing Secret #91: Build a community, not a transaction business.*

9
INFLUENCER MARKETING

No one ever made it big on their own. You need help from others. Doing things on your own is difficult, slow and almost impossible. You don't have enough time to do everything on your own and even if you did, getting someone influential to recommend your product is just so much easier and quicker.

Influencers boost your credibility and send you a storm of traffic at the same time.

Imagine, someone influential telling his 100,000 fans to buy your product or to follow you – if only 1% took action, that's 1,000 new people that visit your website who may convert into customers or subscribers – which would have usually taken you weeks, months or even years to acquire without an influencer. Think of influencer marketing as your fast track to success!

92. Treating Influencers like Robots

Influencers are humans just like you and me. They have feelings. If you praise them, they will be happy. If you insult them, they will feel a bit sad (although they probably got used to it).

- If you help them, they'll help you back. Just like any other person, you meet. If you continuously give them all the time, they'll feel indebted. At some point, they'll be waiting for you to ask them for something. But, you have to help them. Don't just help them once and then expect something in return...build a relationship through continuous help, then ask later. I know it's time consuming especially if you want to connect with several influencers. For that reason, I recommend you start with 20 influencers because frankly, not all of them will reply to your email. To make things easier, here's some guidelines...

- Don't connect with celebrity status influencers – they probably have a secretary doing their email.

- Make sure they have a twitter account – it's where influencers share links to your and stuff. (YouTube and other platforms will be useful too, depending on what you want to promote).

- Stick with the 10,000 - 50,000 twitter followers range – although twitter followers isn't a measure of how much engagement they get. (check statuspeople.com to find our if their followers are real)

- Give, give, give, give, give, give, give, give, give, ask. Give, give, give, give, give, give, give, ask. Just like you should do with customers.
- Keep your messages short and concise.
- Don't ask for something that takes up a lot of their time.
- If an influencer doesn't reply after a few tries, just cross him off the list and look for another one... they'll know you later when you're famous.
- Don't connect with influencers unless you're sure their audience resonates with your... check what they share and promote on social media. Do the things they share seem close to what you want them to share? Would you like their audience to become your customers?
- There is always a way to help them... you just need to find it. (Just kidding, I'll tell you some in the next point).

Action Plan

Write down your list of 20 influencers, join their email list, connect with them on social media and watch them. They'll make a mistake or go through a problem at some point. When they do, jump on that chance to help them fix it.

> **Undefeated Marketing Secret #92: Influencers are like customers – if you help them, they'll help you.**

93. Playing The Short Game

Influencer marketing isn't a short term game. It's a long game and if you chose to grow your startup with the help of influencers you must become friends with them first (unless you pay them of course).

Actually if you want to just pay them check out famebit.com, they could help with your product going viral... give it a go.

But, other than that... if you want them to promote your stuff for free, you'll need a long term strategy and have to help for free too. Things become easier when influencers are your friends. You can't do everything on your own and you probably don't have the budget to keep paying influencers all the time.

Let me put it this way; if your best friend for 25 years became a celebrity and you asked them to help promote your product, you think they help you?

Of course! You're there lifelong friend... why wouldn't they?

But, let's assume none of your friends are walking their way towards the influential path. You can go to existing influencers, help them and become friends... don't ask for anything in return just be friends.

Before you ask... here are a few ways you can help influencers...

- Respond to questions they ask to their email subscribers (that means you have to be on their email list).
- Share their content.
- Send them an ego booster email. Such as, "Your Rock!", "You Changed my Life" etc.

- Engage with them on social media.
- Comment on their blogs.
- Tell them about broken links on their website.
- Make something for them or offer to improve their website, eBooks, content etc.
- Write for their blogs.

Action Plan

Build a relationship with influencers who have fans that match your buyer persona.

> *Undefeated Marketing Secret #93: Long term Friendships with influencers is the key to fast growth.*

94. Reaching Out With a Non-Empathetic Generic Template

I've done this. In fact, when I wanted contributions for this book, I did it. I didn't do it with everyone, but only those I didn't know…. Which was the majority anyway – but I wanted to test if it was true…

It was true… many influencers smelt a generic template and most of them ignored.

Let's assume the email you write isn't generic, you still need to answer the golden question, "why should they reply to my email?"

And you better have a great explanation; otherwise, you won't get a reply.

To start off, you need to open your email differently just like a blog post except shorter. Empathize with them... you could say something like;

HEY INFLUENCER,
I know you get a TON of emails from [black] asking for [blank]. So, I'll make it quick...
When you start off like that, it shows that you're appreciative and understanding. And since you said you'll make it quick, they'll give you a few more seconds of their time.
In the body, you need to be extremely clear and brief. Don't dive too deep into what you want and don't speak in an indirect way - they know you want something from them - so be honest and straight.
Then end your email with a short question asking them if they would like to participate in your promotional campaign, so you can send them more details.
In the end, everyone is different and there are many ways to do it. Some influencers respond to good offers, some only respond to people they know. You'll just have to go through a bit of trial and error, but in the end it is well worth it.

Action Plan

Be empathetic in your influencer outreach emails. Generic cold emails don't work with people who get hundreds of them every day. I've mentioned it a million time in this book... be different. But, writing an empathetic email isn't enough - you also need a great product - since influencers won't promote crappy things.

> *Undefeated Marketing Secret #94: Send empathetic emails with strong offers they can't refuse.*

10
MISTAKES OF 23
ENTREPRENEURS

I asked each entrepreneur this question...
What's the biggest marketing mistake you've ever made
that's worth warning other entrepreneurs about?
Here are their uncut answers...

Wasting time with freeloaders

"Every audience has them. That's okay. As a business owner, you want to make sure you set up a system so that there is no chance they can waste your time, money, or energy. Get that straight, and everything else becomes easier because you'll be able to focus on the people who want change and are willing to invest in themselves to make it happen."

Tom Morkes (twitter: @tmorkes)
www.insurgentpublishing.com

"Biggest marketing mistake ever was positioning myself as "The Autoresponder Guy." Meaning my focus was positioning myself based on what I did instead of positioning myself on who I helped. If I could do it all over again, instead of becoming The Autoresponder Guy I would have become The Email Marketing for Ecommerce Guy, which is what I'm doing now. So when you're thinking of positioning, its incredibly important, but don't do it based on what you do, base it on who you help because that's the important part."

John McIntyre (twitter: @JohnMcIntyre_)
www.reengager.com

"The biggest marketing mistake I made was NOT doing it. When I was writing my book while working as a marketing consultant I had a mental divide in my head where I was applying my marketing skills to my clients' projects, but not my own because mine were "special" or "not like that." I think this is particularly dangerous for artist/artisan types who feel their work is above marketing. The result of that thinking is simply not being able to impact others with your work and not being able to pay yourself."

Taylor Pearson (twitter: @TaylorPearsonMe)
TaylorPearson.me & TheEndOfJobsBook.com

"Biggest marketing mistake I have ever made was featuring someone that had bad press. Luckily the feature didn't gain too much attention, however it definitely went down as a strong learning lesson. If someone has bad press around them, best to stay away from being associated with them!"

Nathan Chan (twitter: @NathanHChan)
www.foundrmag.com

"Really, there's no big marketing mistakes I've made that entrepreneurs should be wary of. In the age of the Internet, marketing is best making smart micro tests, then launching, learning, and reiterating.

That said, that's not to say I've never made mistakes, especially when it comes to influencer marketing. From writing emails that don't get to the point to always asking more from others. I wrote about the mistakes I've made in more detail in my guide to influencer marketing.

Perhaps the biggest thing I've learned since writing the guide is that building a long-term relationship is 10x more valuable than doing something for one-and-done. Find ways to get to know them, you know, like a person. What's the best way to begin to build a relationship? Often, I've found it's by getting their email and having a conversation with them.

How do you find an influencer's email? Here are the 5 strategies and tools I use to find (almost) any email address."

(www.thestorytellermarketer.com/influencer-marketing-guide)

Jason Quey (twitter: @jdquey)
www.thestorytellermarketer.com

"So I don't know if this qualifies as truly marketing but I think it does because pricing is fundamentally marketing.

My biggest mistake was charging too little. When I began my consulting business, my boss at the time and best friend both told me the best business advice I've ever received.

They told me to take whatever I thought I was worth and double or triple it. So, of course, I didn't do that with my first client. But I have not made that mistake since.

Pricing is marketing because if you value yourself too low (and most people do), you can't effectively market yourself. You also have to justify a higher price. It should be a price that makes you pause and think "am I truly worth this much?"

If the answer isn't yes, don't charge less. Find another business."

Matt McWilliams (twitter: @MattMcWilliams2)
www.mattmcwilliams.com

"The biggest mistake I ever made was marketing a service for a solution that I was in love with the market didn't feel they had a problem that my solution would solve.

As a business owner and marketer, I needed to fall in the love with the problem (and one the market feels is a problem) and not the solution. Unless your prospects see/feel the problem it doesn't matter how well you market the solution."

Greg Hickman (twitter: @gjhickman)
system.ly

"There's free advice, and then there's the advice you pay for. Be careful with both.

A startup, that I am involved with, met several venture capital firms. The purpose was to demo the alpha version of their product and ask for an investment. The VCs seemed to love it. Some wisely recommended going to market with that alpha product right away. They were a bit skeptical and wanted to see product/ market fit.

The team, hungry for investment and validation, listened to this advice. They developed an eCommerce website to sell the alpha product. The strategy had limited success.

Why? The alpha product focused only on the end of their customers' buyer journey. The team knew that. They had the right vision. They understood the buyer journey, it was obvious. Yet they also wanted the approval of these "wise" VCs. The funny thing is that NONE of those VCs ever invested. What a waste of time! The price was months handed over to poor advice, given by people who had no skin in the game. With a refreshed focus, the product roadmap is back on track. There is real traction from customers. There is real traction with a different set of investors, the last round is complete. No surprise, those who provided dollars, also provided deal flow and the best advice."

Bryan Eisenberg (twitter: @TheGrok)
www.bryaneisenberg.com

"Trying to be everywhere will get you no where My biggest mistake was trying to be everywhere when I was first starting off. I'd read an article about some strategy to get traffic or some way to make money, and I'd do that, or I'd hear from a friend about their success on one platform and I'd immediately setup an account. However, trying to be everywhere meant I was getting no where. Every time I'd pivot to something else, I'd lose momentum and ultimately waste my time. I'd even get frustrated because everyone else was successful. However, it was at that point I learned something extremely valuable: choose your one thing and master it. The people you read about, the ones getting over 600K unique visitors or making big bucks, they mastered a technique when they first started off. They didn't get there by just trying everything and putting a little effort into a bunch of things. Instead they chose one thing and they nailed it. Choose your one thing and master that. The rest will just fall into place."

Dave Chesson (twitter: @DaveChesson)
Kindlepreneur.com

"The biggest marketing mistake that I've ever made is being too reliant on a single marketing channel. I ran a network of personal finance blogs between 2007 and 2011 called American Consumer News that received more than 50% of its web traffic from Google search results. In early 2011, Google dramatically changed their search algorithm and almost every personal finance website got hammered in the ranks. More than half of my web-

traffic disappeared overnight and I was in a really tight position because I hadn't bothered researching and finding other marketing channels that worked.I firmly believe that no one marketing channel should make up any more than 25% of your business because your business will take a seriously blow if your primary marketing channel disappears."

Matt Paulson (twitter: @MatthewDP)
www.Marketbeat.com

"My blog is the most important part of my marketing efforts since it is real estate I own. Unlike my social feeds like Twitter, I control my blog. However, I chose a crappy name and URL for the blog. "Web Ink Now" sounded clever at the time but is meaningless. I wish I had chosen something more descriptive of what I write about -- Marketing and Sales Strategies."

David Meerman Scott (twitter: @dmscott)
www.webinknow.com

"Focusing on mainstream media. Offline media doesn't convert that well to online. I know tons of people that have built these big careers doing traditional media and they try to get their audience back to the web/email/etc and they fail big time. It's not just flipping a switch and your fan base migrates. People fail to understand that."

Jordan Harbinger (twitter: @theartofcharm)
www.theartofcharm.com

"The biggest marketing mistake I have ever made is scaling way too fast. With marketing, especially when you're spending dollars to acquire customers....you want to scale slowly. There was a time where I figured out that for every $1 I put in marketing I would get $3 back and it seemed like I was just going to mint money from that point forward. However, the more you spend on marketing....things tend to change. You hit equilibrium points, your campaigns get broader and your conversions may not always stay the way they were to start. Instead of dumping a massive amount of money when you figure out a marketing strategy, scale slowly and keep tracking/testing your results. Not only will you save a lot of headache by doing this, you can save yourself from potentially losing a lot of money."

Jeet Banerjee (@TheJeetBanerjee)
www.JeetBanerjee.com

"I think the biggest mistake entrepreneurs tend to make—early on, especially—is failing to build a profitable funnel, and instead relying on non-repeatable one-off circumstances to generate revenue.
We get some early success with our first product, and think "great, now I just have to keep growing those

numbers every month and this thing will take off!"
What entrepreneurs often don't realize is that
they've burned through their buyers, and don't have
a way to get more business from them, nor do they
have a way to get more customers quickly enough.

This is especially true for bloggers who build a
mailing list by offering great content, then launch a
product, only to find that when they try to do it again
the next month, they've already sold their one
product to everyone who's going to buy—in an
audience that took years to build. Instead of cranking
away to put out another product to sell to that same
list, they should be building a profitable funnel that
turns new leads into customers.

Instead, what I wish I'd known from the start was the
importance of building funnels—starting with an
offer in mind, and building out assets to take people
up the pathway from new lead to customer to repeat
customer (ultimately with a subscription or
organizational purchase.)"

Justin Baeder (twitter: @eduleadership)
www.eduleadership.org

"The biggest marketing mistake I ever made was
putting my second book, How to Be an
Imperfectionist, up for pre-order on Amazon. This
isn't inherently a bad idea, but the way I executed it
sure was! I put my book up for sale two months
before release. I gained 420 pre-orders in that time—
not bad—but when launch time came, I had already
exhausted much of my marketing power. For books
especially, the first days of release are the most

Z a k   M u s t a p h a

important! It's also worth mentioning that Amazon adjusts your sales ranking whenever the sale is made, so instead of a concentrated boom of sales on launch day to shoot my book up the charts, my 420 sales were weakened by being spread out over a period of two months.

This insight obviously applies to book marketing, but the concept can apply to all of business: know when (and when not) to push for the sale. If you ask for the sale too soon, you risk alienating a customer that needs to be warmed up first. If you wait too long to ask for the sale (or don't ask at all), you risk the customer losing interest. It's a skill to be able to know when and how to ask for the sale of any product. I'm still learning, but I can say for certain that book sales in particular are best saved for launch or just before launch unless you have the following of Stephen King. For most authors, you might want to leave the pre-order option alone."

Stephen Guise (twitter: @deepexistence)
www.deepexistence.com & www.minihabits.com

"The biggest marketing mistake I ever made was assuming that I could help everyone right from the beginning.

When I first started my internet marketing business (because it was via the internet) I thought I could help any business become successful online and so I set up Facebook advertising targeting small business owners in the United States . . . way too large of a target market. By targeting this wide array of individuals I wasted valuable advertising dollars and more importantly, time, energy and focus.

It was a valuable learning experience and so I wouldn't change anything, but I've since realized that identifying a specific target market has helped me to become a sought out resource for internet marketing.

Currently, I've identified two areas at which I'm currently able to offer the most value to others. The first is in the golf industry. With my book, The Social Golf Course, I've become the go to expert on social media marketing for golf courses. Identifying this clear target market has helped focus my efforts, secure speaking engagements and land more clients. The second is local small and medium-sized businesses. I've become very active in my local community and am the current Chairman of the Board for the Chino Valley Chamber of Commerce. By being the go to resource on anything internet marketing related in our community, I've been able to acquire many new clients, engage with local influencers and have a positive impact on my community.

If I had advice for someone starting a business fresh was to work on identifying a clear target market of customers whom you can be an invaluable resource to and go from there.

As Chris Brogan, a guest on my Defining Success Podcast said, "When I think of ways to make money I fail. When I think of ways to be of service to others, I make money."

Zeb Welborn (twitter: @ZebWelborn)
www.WelbornMedia.com

"My biggest marketing mistake is not understanding the maturity of the market I was selling into. We provide online social media and content marketing training but we found it hard to differentiate from the many competitors in the marketplace. So we created a unique framework called the PRISM funnel which helped us differentiate. P for people, R for relationships, I for inbound traffic, S for subscribers and social retargeting and M for monetization. This unique framework helps us stand out from our competition. Entrepreneurs need to evaluate their market and make sure their product or service is clearly differentiated."

Ian Cleary (twitter: @IanCleary)
www.razorsocial.com

"OVER confidence. I knocked it out of the park with Podcasters' Paradise. 2800 members and 3.5 million in revenue in less than 2 years? I was on top of the world. I thought every product I launched would CRUSH. Two failed products later, I knew I had to PRE-VALIDATE my ideas, or keep failing. With http://TheFreedomJournal.com, I pre-sold 100 copies just as an IDEA. It was THEN I knew I had something. The verdict? I launched via Kickstarter on January 4th, raised over 400k, and became the 5th most

funded publishing campaign of ALL TIME on Kickstarter. Summation? Over confidence loses. Pre-validation wins."

John Lee Dumas (twitter: @johnleedumas)
www.eofire.com

"The most expensive mistake is **working with the wrong people.** There are three ways to make this mistake and they will all cost you money in varying amounts. Here they are:

Working with the wrong clients or customers
They're more expensive to service, and even if you get it right, they're not very happy. It's usually one of three problems:
They aren't paying you as much as you need to do great work.
They need you to do things faster than you normally can, and quality suffers.
They ask you do something that isn't your main service or core strength
Sometimes, you choose these customers because you're hungry. Or maybe you just liked them. Sometimes, it's because you thought it would lead to referrals. But it doesn't work because you weren't able to be your best.

Hiring the wrong candidate
This is a classic mistake. They seemed like the right person for the job. You tried to make it work. You

even adapted the job to fit the person. But nothing works. There are usually two problems.

Not a culture fit: They don't work we'll on the team or with the customers. They don't communicate well and it's causing an emotional backlash for everyone. Not a skill fit: They don't have the horsepower or knowledge to do the job at the level you require. Everyone likes them, but everyone has to pick up slack.

The key to avoiding these issues is to go slow, involve the team and to hire for strengths, not for lack of weakness. Look for people who solve problems, not people who have answers."

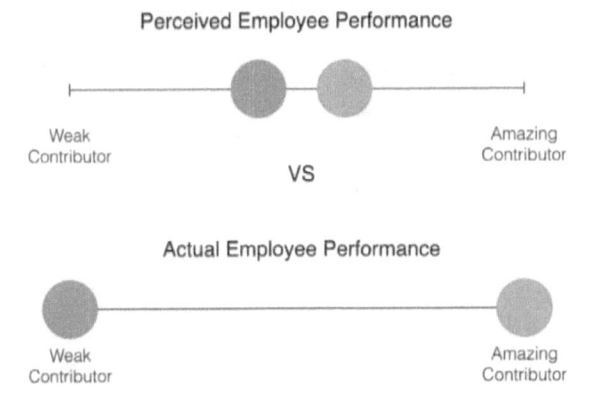

(Image credit: https://medium.com/swlh/how-to-hire-34f4ded5f176)

Finally, that brings us to the biggest mistake

Choosing the Wrong Business Partner
Nothing is more toxic to a culture, more harmful to moral or more deadly to your strategy. Having the wrong person as an equity partner will pull your

focus and marketing off course every day. You can't build high with cracks in the foundation."

Andy Crestodina (twitter: @crestodina)
www.orbitmedia.com

Not building an email list.

"When I first started blogging, I'd hear about how important it was to grow my following on social networks. So I added Twitter widgets, Facebook widgets and all sorts of things in the hope of growing my following. What I came to learn was that I was just giving people a reason to leave my blog and get distracted by cat videos.

As soon as I shifted my focus to building my email list, things changed. Email has a far higher ROI and it has a higher traffic potential.
When Facebook changed its newsfeed algorithm, it proved that we need to use a channel that isn't like building on rented land. I'm not saying don't bother with social. You should, but there are better ways to grow your social following.
Offer an "opt-in bribe" and give them a big reason to subscribe. "Free updates" won't cut it. Once they're in, use your confirmation page & email auto responder to encourage people to connect with you on your favorite social networks."

Adam Connell (twitter: @adamjayc)
www.bloggingwizard.com/blog

"Hold people accountable for progress as well as product. What I mean by that is ensure that the partners and employees you're trusting to complete big tasks frequently communicate progress and status along the way. Do not assume they'll take care of the whole thing and you can trust it will just get done. You have to at least have an eye over the shoulder periodically to ensure you don't become the victim of someone's procrastination, laziness or incompetence. I trusted a friend (which is another problem sometimes) to complete a fairly large sales project for me once. It almost cost me my whole business. He just wasn't capable of delivering and I let my personal trust in him cloud my judgement of the professional side of him. Hold people accountable all along the way and you'll avoid that."

Jason Falls (twitter: @JasonFalls)
www.jasonfalls.com

"The biggest mistake is not maintaining the core AND looking to the future.
We have always maintained the core. But sometimes the future seems too overwhelming, so you bury your head in the sand. It's definitely a mistake.
Both worlds must exist simultaneously."

Sean D'Souza (twitter: @seandsouza)
www.psychotactics.com

"The biggest marketing mistake that myself, and other entrepreneurs I've seen make, is treating social media platforms like advertising mediums.

Traditional marketing for entrepreneurs and solopreneurs was to buy ads in places like newspapers, yellow pages, and other publications. Perhaps even a TV or radio spot. And those ads had to be designed to entice and interest quickly, as there were always limitations. Your budget would limit you to 2 column inches or 30 seconds, or one billboard along the side of the highway.

But social media doesn't work like that.

Businesses can't just broadcast out the same kinds of ads and enticements to Facebook or Twitter and expect their audience to respond, or to even have an audience.

Instead, businesses need to approach social media from the mindset of where and how users are using it. People do not check their Facebook feed to be sold to. They check it to catch up with family and friends, to see what else is going on in the world, to participate in larger conversations.

And it's those larger conversations where savvy businesses are able to make social work for them. Entrepreneurs can pay attention to what other people are talking about and jump into the conversations that are most interesting and relevant, just as you might if you were mingling at a party. The truly smart entrepreneurs start those conversations and build audiences around relevant topics to their business and goals. They don't broadcast to social. They treat social platforms as opportunities to connect with and form relationships with their prospects and customers."

Mike Allton (twitter: @Mike_Allton)
www.sitesell.com

11
FINAL WORDS

W hat you learnt in this book won't do you any good. It's applying what you learnt that will. Read all the secrets, books and study from the best in the world if you can and see if it'll make the slightest difference. Most people will just move to the next book after reading this book and dump this one away because "they are done, reading it". You haven't! You've just started!

Go over the framework in this book and read it several times until you engrave everything in your head.

Learning all the techniques in martial arts isn't what makes you a real black belt. It's the control, speed and mastery of it... sure you could call yourself a black belt if you know all the techniques but it won't do you any good in a real fight will it?

When I first started my driving lessons... in the first 10 seconds, my driving instructor looked at me and said, "Have you done this before?" I told him "no" because I hadn't, however I did play driving games on PlayStation so I knew it theoretically. YET, my driving instructor still made me do another 15 – 18 lessons because I wasn't ready for the real road. I know some people may have taken longer to learn driving but that doesn't matter. What matters most is continuing to practice. Most people give up after the first failure, some on the second, some on the 10th, while others are still working hard after the 10,000th failure.

So, tell me… are you going to give up and move onto the next "exiting" book?

BONUSES

Download the bonus material at:

http://www.foolishnessfile.com/undefeated-marketing-bonus

YOUR WORD MATTERS

I'm glad you've made it this far. I hope you found the book helpful. Most importantly, I hope you do something with it.

Anyway, for the book to spread and help others... I need you to review it on Amazon. If you can do that, I and many other readers will be forever grateful.

Never underestimate the power of your word. Your word matters!

ANY QUESTIONS?

If you felt that I didn't explain some points very well or something was missing or whatever other questions you have about the book then please let me know. I will answer your question directly and also add it in to the bonus material as FAQs so everyone else can benefit.

Please don't be shy to email me at zak@foolishnessfile.com with your questions.

Z a k   M u s t a p h a

ENDNOTES

1. https://managewp.com/14-surprising-statistics-about-wordpress-usage
2. http://www.briantracy.com/blog/time-management/plan-ahead-and-increase-productivity/
3. http://www.huffingtonpost.com/2015/06/02/mea l-planning-will-make-your-life-better_n_7484278.html
4. http://fourhourworkweek.com/2014/07/21/harry s-prelaunchr-email/
5. http://offers.hubspot.com/2014-state-of-inbound
6. https://www.nngroup.com/articles/f-shaped-pattern-reading-web-content/
7. http://www.copyblogger.com/increase-blog-subscribers/
8. https://www.quicksprout.com/2015/04/13/7-lessons-learned-by-publishing-300-guest-posts/
9. Jon Morrow's GuestBlogging.com Course.
10. The Copywriter's Handbook by Bob Bly
11. http://optinmonster.com/how-it-works/
12. http://www.ncbi.nlm.nih.gov/pubmed/22869334
13. http://www.ncbi.nlm.nih.gov/pubmed/9569648
14. http://wearesocial.com/uk/blog/2014/08/global-social-media-users-pass-2-billion
15. http://www.bloomberg.com/bw/stories/2008-09-16/why-zappos-offers-new-hires-2-000-to-quitbusinessweek-

Zak   Mustapha

Notes

Notes

www.ingramcontent.com/pod-product-compliance
Lightning Source LLC
Chambersburg PA
CBHW020904180526
45163CB00007B/2623